Sober in Seven

Transform Your Drinking With This Radical New Guide

Andy Smith

Grosvenor House
Publishing Limited

This book is published by
Grosvenor House Publishing Ltd
Link House
140 The Broadway, Tolworth, Surrey, KT6 7HT.
www.grosvenorhousepublishing.co.uk

A CIP record for this book
is available from the British Library

ISBN 978-1-78623-698-2

Disclaimer:

This book is not a substitute for medical advice or support.
The principles contained within this programme are based on proven
methodologies such as Neuro-linguistic Programming, Cognitive Behavioural
Therapy, Thought Field Therapy and commercial business coaching
approaches applied through a ton of life experience.

Thousands of people have used what you are about to read to reclaim
their lives from alcohol addiction, but there is no one approach to
fit every situation, so individual results will vary.

Acknowledgements

I dedicate this book to everyone who has been part of my journey on this wonderful, tragic, beautiful, painful and amazing thing we call life.

In particular I dedicate it to my wonderful and beautiful partner Louise and my children Megan, Oliver and Joshua. Your unending patience on this occasionally self-indulgent voyage of self-discovery has been nothing short of miraculous. Through the often-painful process of growth, I have obtained a sense of why I was put on this planet and I get to change people's lives each day.

I am the epitome of the phrase, *'In order to be old and wise, first you must be young and stupid'*, and that has been tough on everyone at times. Mum and Dad, I give thanks for your love and counsel every day. Born in your heart, not under it.

Contents

Sober in Seven

Your journey to a better life starts here.

Introduction

Hey there! My name is Andy, and, if you don't know a very important fact about me, it is that I can't stand theoretical solutions from so-called 'professional experts'. People who may have letters after their name, but no clue about what it really means to suffer, or to transcend that suffering.

The suffering I speak of is, of course, that brought about by alcohol addiction.

This book is different. If you could use a road map to follow to completely reprogramme your feelings about alcohol, then this is it. So relax, because you are in the right place.

What this book _isn't_:

- a relentless regurgitation of buzzwords and theory about addiction
- a simple recount of my own experience, along the lines of 'Look how bad it was for me, and how great it is now'. (Although I will share relevant aspects of this to give context and motivation around what you are about to learn)

- a simple piece of 'quit-lit' designed to frivolously promote 'sober living'. (I can't believe these are *actual* terms these days)
- a 'heard it before' summary of what is out there already. Yes, I quote some relevant 'universal truths' but there is genuinely ground breaking new information in here which **works**.

What this book *is:*

- a <u>proven</u>* way to switch off your feelings about alcohol if you follow the process
- based on *proven influencing psychology* from a record-breaking career in selling, influencing and coaching across the healthcare spectrum
- an enjoyable way to remove the main obstacle standing between you and your dreams
- a way to enjoy better physical and mental health, better relationships, have more energy and productivity and to save $£*thousands*, every year for the rest of your life.

* The online programme has a money-back guarantee. At the time of writing, the refund rate was less than 0.5%

How to get the best out of this book:

Get over to:

https://soberinseven.com/bookresources

RIGHT NOW and put your details in.

I will *immediately* send you a ton of really cool stuff for FREE.

Put the book down, open your browser and do this now – it will bring this whole journey to life for you. There are audios, videos and there is also a facility to book some one-to-one time with me personally if you want to chat!

This journey is not just about getting control of your drinking, this is a journey of personal growth, and I will start sharing these tools with you.

Carve out some time, and binge on the book and the content I have sent you via email. Devote your very soul to this over the next few days and it will fundamentally change your life <u>for the better *forever*</u>.

I don't write this for awards or recognition. I write this to help you be your best self. I write this out of anger and frustration at the *utter lack* of viable and reliable self-help methodologies available, if we find ourselves in the alcohol trap (much more on that later).

I write this because, now, in my sixth decade, I understand exactly why I was put on this planet – to help YOU, right NOW.

3

> *'Thank you, Andy – you really are the only credible alternative to Alcoholics Anonymous (AA).*
>
> *I went to one of their meetings with a friend and knew it wasn't for me. This is a real one-stop shop. Not only have you 'been there', you also know the route out of this. You can't teach someone to swim if you have never gotten wet yourself!'*
>
> Hazel, USA

Have you ever seen the movie *Slumdog Millionaire*? The film won eight of the ten Academy Awards™ it was nominated for in 2009 and told the story of Jamal Malik, a teenage Indian boy living in the slums of Mumbai who becomes a contestant on the popular TV quiz show, 'Who wants to be a Millionaire?' The premise of the show, if you haven't seen it, is that you answer fifteen questions in ascending order of difficulty and value until after the final one, you win twenty million rupees.

To everyone's amazement, Jamal begins to answer the questions correctly. He is detained by the police and accused of cheating and he recounts how some of the extraordinary hardship he has endured in his life, has given him the answers to these questions.

You see, even in the darkest moments of your life, you have been building the strength you need to beat this addiction. Read that statement again. Underline it if you must, as it is a universal TRUTH. The person you are right now has all the tools you need to put alcohol firmly in its place and rise above your current circumstances. You just need someone to show you how to piece it all together. And that is *exactly* what I am going to do.

Before I do, consider this. If you and I were to play poker, and you didn't understand the rules, you would lose. It wouldn't even matter if you had the entire deck of cards in your hand, if you didn't know what a Royal Flush or a Full House looked like, the cards would be meaningless and your chances of success virtually nil, save for the extremely slim chance of a *coincidence*. By understanding the rules of the game, you begin to understand the cards that play in your favour, and those that will count against you and thus need to be mitigated.

This therapeutic process is exactly the same. By understanding the assets you have in your favour, and the obstacles you need to prepare for, *success becomes the likely outcome*, rather than failure, even if you have tried and failed countless times before. (The vast majority of people doing the online FREEDOM programme have tried Alcoholics Anonymous (AA), Hypnotherapy or counselling, and yet the success rate transcends all of those approaches.)

Try to think of unlocking your feelings around alcohol as a combination lock with say, twenty numbers in it. Maybe you have three of those numbers right now, or maybe you have nineteen. Either way, the outcome is the same – the lock remains firmly shut.

If you were to try to break into the Bank of England or Fort Knox, surely the easiest way to do it would be to have the right combination for the lock and the security codes. If you don't, what are the alternatives? drills? hammers? cutting torches? dynamite? Not only are these approaches dangerous, they also risk destroying that which you seek.

Remember this the next time someone says 'Willpower is what you need' or 'Just drink less' or 'Stop when you have had enough' – they are completely missing the point. And that brings me to the first piece of 'advice' I will give you:

Read the whole book, and do <u>all</u> of the exercises.

I am willing to bet this is important to you, so consider this a one-off project to deal with this for *good*.

Some parts will be a genuine revelation, and some may feel a bit more like, 'Yeah, I think I knew that'.

Remember the combination lock – you already have some of the numbers, so take time to remind yourself of that, before moving to the next section.

By the end of this book, I expect you to have scrawled all over it, made copious notes and have underlined key parts of it that really stand out for you. These are your missing numbers for the combination lock.

This combination lock has a lot of numbers and is unique and personal to you. While some of those numbers are small, they are ALL important in this process, so if something resonates with you, acknowledge and record it by writing it down. This transfers the learning much more quickly to your subconscious mind.

This approach is applicable to **you**. I know you are too smart to fall into the *'It's alright for you'* or *'My life is different'* trap. I have dealt with people who have been abused, betrayed and have suffered unimaginable loss and grief, but also people who are completely bewildered about how they find themselves in this situation, as their life is otherwise great and they feel there is something deeply wrong with them for falling into the trap of alcohol dependence and addiction.

There is nothing wrong with them, or you.

Life is sometimes really hard, and alcohol is portrayed in society as a solution in the most random of instances.

Got something to celebrate? Drink alcohol.
It's your birthday? Drink alcohol.
Not feeling courageous? Drink alcohol.
Feeling sad? Drink alcohol.
Feeling happy? Drink alcohol.
Feeling anxious? Drink alcohol.
Feeling lonely? Drink alcohol.
Feeling loved? Drink alcohol.
Feeling unloved? Drink alcohol.
Feeling stressed? Drink alcohol.
Feeling tired and need to sleep? Drink alcohol.
Feeling relieved it's the weekend? Drink alcohol.
Feel like your boss hates you? Drink alcohol.
Feeling let down by someone? Drink alcohol.
It's the weekend? Drink alcohol.
Had a tough day at work? Drink alcohol.
Bored? Drink alcohol.

If alcohol *actually* helped with any of these things, the world would feel like a fundamentally different place, wouldn't it?

I am sure you probably read all those with a wry smile on your face, but I repeat those words for a very important reason:

> Alcohol dependence resides in your **FEELINGS**
> and the social pressure to consume it is *relentless*.

So before you dive in to the main part of the book, remember that this approach is different.

'If you do what you have always done, you will get what you've always got'

–Tony Robbins

Or perhaps the great Albert Einstein said it better:

'Problems cannot be solved with the same mindset that created them.'

So, be prepared to be challenged, have some long-held beliefs smashed and to <u>enjoy the ride</u>. The only entry tickets for your exciting future are an open mind and a willingness to learn!

Do we have a deal?

Yes?

Then let's get started…

11 hrs · 🌐   •••

I wake up in the middle of the night, head pounding and gasping for water, trying to figure out how I got here! I get up and go downstairs, trying not to wake the household, so I can have a glass of water. Every time I think not again, tomorrow I'll change, im not drinking tomorrow! I go back to bed.

Morning comes round and it's time to get the kids breakfast and get ready for the school run, I still have a banging headache! How can I drive the kids to school when I know I'm probably still over the limit and how can I go to work when I feel this rough!! I'm never drinking again!!!

Lunch time comes round and I'm feeling much better, Mc Donald's run?!? Of course why not, I need something naughty after a night on the wine! Afternoon at work goes steady, I'm full of Maccys and feel great! A few hours later, heading over to do the afternoon school run I think to myself- what shall I do the children for dinner tonight?

Kids in the cars, we're stopping at Tesco to get "something for tea" and a couple of bottles of wine for mummy, after all I've had a long day and now I feel ok, I deserve a bottle or two!

Back to the middle of the night.....

👍😢❤️ 66   48 Comments

'Karen', UK on Facebook.

My 'A-ha' Moment

One day in 2016, I was shopping in our local supermarket for that evening's dinner. I had just come off the telephone with my boss – an obtuse hypocrite and bully of a man, who felt the best way to motivate someone was to continually tell them that what they were doing was not good enough, and if he were in their shoes, he would have made a different decision and the outcome would have been far, far superior. Funnily enough he failed at most things he did!

Now don't get me wrong, I was very confident in my own abilities. I had won prestigious business awards, dramatically turned company performances around across the entire healthcare spectrum, and felt I knew what I was doing.

In fact, the business I had taken over had been declining at thirty per cent and now, just a few months later, we were growing at eighty per cent. This was not a new experience for me, but this was the first time in my life that I felt it was completely pointless. None of my achievements were given the slightest credence, which I found completely dispiriting.

There was a war going on inside my head and I was stressed out. My drinking had reached Olympic levels and I was occasionally consuming up to a *litre* of gin in a sitting, plus wine 'to get me started'. So, while I was pushing my trolley around the supermarket, I suffered my first ever panic attack. My heart started pounding out of my chest, my skin was on fire, and I could feel consciousness starting to slip away fast. To avoid passing out on the floor, I hurriedly stumbled backwards to take a seat in one of the display fridges and waited for my head to clear. A little old lady took time out of her shopping to come over and see this

The FREEDOM Programme:

Chapter 1 – Focus

Getting clear on WHY you want to do this is an extremely critical part of the process. In the testing moments that inevitably come, you need to have something to keep you moving forward. Nobody can give you your 'why' – you have to work it out for yourself.

Right now, you may think you know your WHY but it may not be sufficient to sustain you through lasting change. So why do you want to make a change? You may have had an ultimatum from your spouse, your boss or even your partner.

You may have had the 'hangover to end all hangovers' and you have vowed never to drink again. You may have become abusive or offensive to someone you care about and it is made you question who you really are. Very few, if any, of these reasons will serve as a foundation for what you are trying to achieve, no matter how valid they are right now. But by taking a more structured approach to setting some goals, using a proven coaching model that works in the commercial world, we can build unshakeable motivation by getting really clear about what is in it for you, as well as a full understanding of the consequences of inaction.

Neuro-linguistic Programming (NLP) teaches us about goals which are 'move-towards' or 'move-away'. The situations I have described above are 'move-away' motivators. They are painful experiences which are extremely powerful in creating a desire for change, but they tend not to last. A bad hangover fades over time, and so does the memory of it. Drunken insults get forgiven (if never truly forgotten). Ultimatums and deadlines pass, and if the promised catastrophe doesn't arise, then we get complacent. As we move forward from these moments, their power over us diminishes and over time we drop our guard, old habits re-establish themselves and we are back where we started – or often in a worse place.

If you flip these goals around, then as we get closer to them, they start to become *more* motivational over time. Let me give you an example. I was speaking with a client who was in his sixties. He had been a heavy drinker for most of his life but had also been sporty and active, as well as holding down a physical job as an odd-job man. He was struggling a little with his 'why' and when I probed him on it, he didn't feel unwell, in spite of the fact he was on medication for blood pressure and cholesterol and knew he wasn't helping his health one bit. This lack of a constant 'reminder' that he was killing himself (his words) meant he was struggling with motivation.

When I asked why he felt it was important to stay healthy, he began talking effusively about the prospect of becoming a grandfather for the first time and all that entailed. He spoke at length about his desire to be an active participant in his grandchild's life, for as long as possible, and as he was describing this, I could hear his tone changing. He started to realise his 'move-towards' goal was being a healthy and happy grandfather that could run and play with his young grandchildren.

In that moment, alcohol switched from being the thing that may or may not be damaging his health, to becoming the VERY THING THAT STOOD IN THE WAY OF THIS GOAL! This sounds like a very subtle difference, but it is ENORMOUSLY powerful. To take this a step further, we should set our goals out of love rather than FEAR.

FEAR and move-away goals can be powerful in the short term, but goals set out of LOVE and that are move-towards are immeasurably more powerful in the long run, and make no mistake – this is a lifelong change of thinking. As you run through the programme, keep a hold of your move-away or fear-based goals and write them down. They are probably what made you buy this book, but they are not what will get to where you want to be.

Let's have a little fun with this and run through some examples:

Move-away or fear-based goal	Move-towards or love-based goal
If I don't sort this out, my partner will leave me.	I am going to be the best partner I can be, living a life where love is given without condition and accepted with gratitude.
My health is suffering – I need to change.	I am going to make the best of every day I have on this planet, enjoying every experience to the max because of my energy and vitality.
My drinking is consuming all my spare money.	I pursue endeavours that make me truly happy in my spare time – I continually learn and build strong relationships with those I care about.
I embarrassed myself and said things that really weren't me and I hate myself for it.	I am kind at all times. I think before I speak and am in total control of how I react to others.
I don't want to get fired from my job by being unproductive due to hangovers and lethargy.	I am energised and alive – I get out of my job what I put into it, and feel valued as a result.

Get the idea? Have some fun with this. The huge difference between the two approaches is that love-based goals make you feel like you are the architect of your own future (which you are). And they are WAY more fun.

Over time, as you start to feel these goals becoming reality, you will start to adapt them and stretch yourself further, because you have the confidence in yourself to achieve and exceed them. Fear-based goals, as well as fading are actually quite depressing to hang on to, and we consciously avoid facing them down anyway.

So how to begin this process?

Introducing the **Life Balance Disc.**

The purpose of this exercise is twofold:

1. We get really clear on where we are now. This is super-important as the journey from A to B begins with an accurate realisation of where A actually is. We also develop a much clearer vision on what our 'upside' of making our wonderful decision really is.
2. We start to build our energy levels by building gratitude into our life. Gratitude has one of the highest vibrations and energies of any emotion. By moving away from guilt and shame (the lowest energy emotions) and building in more love, joy and gratitude, we start to raise our overall wellbeing and energy, and it feels *amazing*.

The Life Balance Disc:

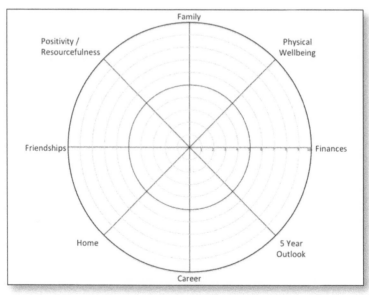

Give this exercise the attention it deserves and don't move on until you have thoroughly completed it. I promise you – this is the ticket to freedom and it will carry you through the inevitable tough moments to come.

Sketch this out on a piece of paper as you will want to repeat this exercise periodically as you go through this journey. You can download a free digital copy included in the resources at https://soberinseven.com/bookresources

Give yourself a score out of ten for each of the areas.

Resist the temptation to mark anything a zero or a ten. If you are breathing, and able to read this book, you have something to be grateful for so not a zero.

Likewise, if you are tempted to give yourself a ten, is it really perfect with no place to improve? If it is, then please tell me how to get there! Let's make sure you are not deluding yourself – there is *always* something that can be better.

Also, when you repeat this exercise, don't see a decreasing number as failure – this is not a race to ten.

As we succeed, our expectations change and we begin to demand more of ourselves. Use the repetition of this exercise to help stimulate your goals for the next three months, for example.

You may well be doing this from a position of feeling quite helpless about your drinking and that is absolutely fine. Over time, when this 'problem' fades into a distant memory, other things will come into your life to challenge you!

Then, make a note of *at least three things* you are grateful for under each heading. This is really important. You will learn why later in the book.

Use the guidance below as a bit of context.

Family:
How is your 'family' functioning? How are your relationships with your partner, parents, siblings, children or other significant family members? Everyone will have a different family structure – large, small, distant, local. How is this feeling? Are there harmonious relationships? Things to forgive? Bridges that need to be rebuilt?

Give yourself a mark out of ten, and a minimum of three things you are grateful for.

Physical wellbeing:
How is your health? Are you feeling young or old for your age? Do you move well and are able to enjoy all the things an active and healthy life affords? Are you on medication for things that would be considered lifestyle-related or preventable, or do you dance out of bed every morning full of energy and ready to take on the challenges of the day ahead, whatever they may be?

Give yourself a mark out of ten, and a minimum of three things you are grateful for.

Finances:
What kind of financial shape are you in? Are you surviving, thriving, keeping your head above water, or sinking without a trace? This area is not simply a matter of the size of your bank balance, this is about the flow of money through your life – are you taking care of your daily needs, planning for the future and also having the resources to enjoy your life, whatever that might look like for you?

Give yourself a mark out of ten, and a minimum of three things you are grateful for.

Five Year Outlook:
As you look ahead, can you see success awaiting on your current trajectory, or are there dark clouds looming? Where do you see yourself in five years' time? Are there positive indicators of good times ahead, or are there small issues now that may grow over time?

Give yourself a mark out of ten, and a minimum of three things you are grateful for.

Career:
We spend a huge portion of our lives earning our wages and providing for our loved ones. It makes sense that it should, at the very least, feel like a worthwhile exercise. Is your career progressing as you would hope? Are there opportunities for growth? Are there risks that need to be managed? Do you dream of starting your own business as a side hustle, with a view to making it your full-time passion?

Give yourself a mark out of ten, and a minimum of three things you are grateful for.

Home:
How is your home environment? Is it a place to feel secure, relaxed and content? Are there countless small jobs that keep getting put off? When you enter your home, how do you feel about it?

Give yourself a mark out of ten, and a minimum of three things you are grateful for.

Friendships:
We humans are social animals. We *need* friendship and companionship. How are those friendships in terms of number,

and also quality? Does your social circle inspire you, or are you a fully paid up member of the 'Ah yes, but' club? Do your friends bring you energy or sap it?

Give yourself a mark out of ten, and a minimum of three things you are grateful for.

Positivity/Resourcefulness:
How do you deal with life's inevitable knocks? Do you allow them to derail you, or do you remain strong and optimistic? Are you good in a crisis, and continually look for alternative approaches when things go wrong? Or do you procrastinate relentlessly and listen to your excuses?

Give yourself a mark out of ten, and a minimum of three things you are grateful for.

Over time you build a picture of the 'shape' of your life, and you may get a real sense of priority around where your real 'upsides' are.

It may look a bit like this:

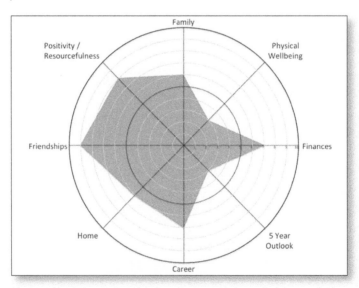

When you have completed this exercise, take the time to note down any reflections that you make. Are there any surprises when you choose to look at this objectively?

> NOW the fun bit... fast forward to a point in the future when you have got alcohol in its proper place – *whatever that looks like for you.*

Repeat this scoring exercise *from that perspective*, and note the numbers on the disc.

Where are the differences? Are they in some of the areas, or all of the areas?

Take note of the differences. What do they represent?

For example, if your health has moved from X to Y. What does that represent? Weight loss? Is your blood pressure coming down? Maybe you have ditched the antidepressants? Make some notes at what jumps out – these are your upsides and **these are the wonderful gifts that you will give yourself** by seeing this process through.

You own these. They are within your grasp.

Now I am generally pretty scathing about the AA 'live a day at a time' approach as it never seems to have an ending, but there is some real truth to it in the early days. Seeing the prize is all well and good, but it can lead to 'overwhelm' so just take it as your destination and nothing more at this stage. This programme is like a satnav, or GPS system in that it knows where you are headed and will help you get there – one step at a time. Trust the process and feel great that you are on your way.

You may have followed my Tour de France blog and have seen the video of me at the top of the Col d'Aubisque in the Pyrenees on the last mountain day – Stage 19. (It's in your free stuff accessed when you put your email address on the website).

At no point during the whole Tour did I allow myself the luxury of thinking I could complete this 'impossible' challenge. I kept my head down all the way through it and simply got to the next food stop, the next hotel and survived to start again another day. This approach helped, as it stopped me completely freaking out and kept me humble and focused. I saw other riders struggle at different times and disaster seemed to be one mis-step away. A careless motorist. Some contaminated water in a mountain spring. Failure or success had a huge element of good fortune wrapped up in it.

However, at the top of the Aubisque, the final, brutal mountain climb of the 2018 Tour de France, I dared believe that I had finally managed it. Only the two stages of the very short Individual Time Trial and the procession into Paris and the Champs-Elysees lay between me and something that had been utterly impossible before. I had some mobile signal on my phone and went 'Live' on Facebook to my followers. I started explaining rationally about what I had done, and where I was. I likened the situation to being 2–0 ahead in a football match, but with four minutes of extra time remaining. For sure, I was in a strong position, but I wasn't done yet. And then a strange thing happened. The tears came like an avalanche. In that very moment, I allowed myself to truly appreciate what I had achieved to get to that point.

I made my excuses about needing to get going to get to the meeting point, and ended the video. I sobbed like a baby for five minutes straight. The emotion was unbelievable. You too will get there. By focusing on the steps between where you are now, and where you want to be, you will get there and you will have your own 'Aubisque moment', when you realise a fundamental shift has been achieved.

But that day is not today.

Sorry.

There is some hard work and some discipline to get you there, but now you know the destination. Stay focused, don't get complacent and manage the ups and downs of this journey, and trust me, there will be plenty.

Onwards and upwards! Let's do this!

Chapter Review:

Are you clear on why you want to do this? If I were to bump into you in the lift, would you be able to tell me, in just a few sentences, why you are changing your approach to alcohol?

What are your biggest upsides and what will it mean to you, and the wider world, for you to realise them?

Who benefits? Of course, you do, but who else?

Your family?

Your (real) friends?

Your co-workers?

Your employees?

Take some time to consider these questions before moving on...

Notes/Reflections

Chapter 2 – Reasons

Why do we drink? We clearly have our reasons. If we didn't have those, we wouldn't do it, pure and simple. We use phrases like, 'it's an old friend', 'I deserve it', or 'a little of what you like does no harm'.

For the avoidance of any doubt, the fact you have read this far means we can debunk the last one almost immediately! But these reasons are valid in our heads and our subconscious has been duped. Remember, the subconscious is extremely powerful (around 80-90% of our mind) but totally gullible – it will believe everything it is told, unless the conscious mind actually puts a barrier up, which it doesn't when the messages encouraging us to drink are so subtle and so prolific. As you go through this chapter, please bear in mind that EVERY DAY, people give up alcohol for GOOD.

Society tells us that we are the outliers, the freaks, the weaklings, when the reverse is true. The weak people are those who – just like us – have those voices inside them telling them that something isn't right and yet cannot summon up the courage to even acknowledge this. And that makes you pretty awesome in my book.

The younger generation is shunning alcohol. They now see it for what it is. Universities are closing bars, and getting completely smashed is no longer 'cool'. In fact, my theory on this is twofold: Firstly, they have a new addiction, and it is in the form of a shiny rectangle with an Apple or an Android logo. They are a connected generation in a way that none of us have ever dealt with before. This brings its own issues, which we are only just beginning to realise, but for them it is sure chasing alcohol off the radar.

Secondly, when I was growing up, we would all go out, get completely shitfaced and make all kinds of fools of ourselves. And not in a good way. And there is barely a shred of evidence of what I got up to. Nobody carried cameras and we were all able to kid ourselves that we had 'had a great night' and were 'on it'. The reality of course was completely different. Arguments were started, people were crying and injuries were sustained through aggression or misadventure. We were all complicit in whitewashing the whole thing as 'just a bit of fun' and 'what having a great time looked like'. Now things are different. If a teenager gets incapably drunk, there are people ready with smartphones to record the evidence.

Thus, there is REAL jeopardy to getting out of control. Passing out on the bathroom floor has gone from being 'one of those things' to a social media viral phenomenon, along with the associated humiliation. Also, the feedback loop has been broken. We are now able to see the bloodshot, sweaty, dishevelled reality of a big night out. And your subconscious realises that this doesn't look like quite as much fun as we kidded ourselves it would be.

For people older than teenagers, we are still reaping the false conspiracy that alcohol equals fun, and it is causing misery to millions. Some people – like you – have woken up to the madness that is going on around us and others remain trapped by their own ignorance. Every day, I get people who contact me with a whole narrative around why they drink, why it's someone else's fault, and why someone should convince them otherwise. They are what I call the 'Go ahead, fix me, then' brigade.

And then I get emails from people just like you, who are proactive and willing to take some action, as they know that they are better than this. They are willing to challenge themselves, invest in themselves and make a brave decision without being one hundred per cent sure what the outcome may look like.

> **Your days of carefree drinking are over – you know too much.**

As you read this, you may be feeling a sense of dread in that what you held dear is not what you thought and there may be no sign of an alternative but don't worry – this is a good thing, and in fact shows you are ready to embrace some new thinking.

So, before we go any further, you need to understand that alcohol is an addictive substance – just like nicotine, crack cocaine, heroin and crystal meth. We have little problem accepting these as being so nowadays, and yet alcohol has managed to slip through the fingers of this kind of categorisation.

When you ask drinkers about the implications, you tend to get the following perceptions:
Harmful? Yes.
It impairs judgment? Of course.
Creates huge social issues? Yes. (But not them of course...☺)
Addictive? Errrr... maybe?

There is simply not enough social acceptance of alcohol being an addictive drug for it to really have gained that categorisation, but that doesn't make it true. If you met someone at a party and they told you they worked for a tobacco company, researching into new ways to make their products more accessible to children and younger people, you would probably have quite a visceral reaction to that. If that same person told you they were head of marketing for alcopops, you probably wouldn't have the same view, even though their jobs are ostensibly the same – getting people addicted early, in the full knowledge that societal pressure will take care of everything else.

In fact, by relative addictive effect, alcohol is second only to heroin in its addictive effect on dopamine levels in the brain, making us want more.

Most addictive substances:

1. Heroin
2. **Alcohol**
3. Cocaine
4. Barbiturates
5. Nicotine

Nutt et al, 2007

A recent survey found that twenty-five per cent of adults found their drinking made them unhappy and made them feel the need to make a change. A further survey found that thirty-three per cent of drinkers stated that alcohol created problems at home in some way or another. Do you still think that the notion that alcohol is 'harmless fun' stacks up?

If you are anything like me, you knew that this was probably true anyway, and yet chose to disregard it – this is called *cognitive dissonance*.

> Cognitive dissonance refers to a situation involving conflicting attitudes, beliefs or behaviours. This produces a feeling of mental discomfort leading to an alteration in one of the attitudes, beliefs or behaviours to reduce the discomfort and restore balance.

We tend to latch on to attitudes and beliefs that remove or reduce this discomfort. For example, we drink in spite of the fact that it can make us acutely unhappy and will latch on to the belief that it is a reward, a necessary means of relaxation or simply how you cope with your boss/partner/kids/workload, etc. If this reduces the feeling of conflict, it is adopted as the perceived reality, even if it is blatantly untrue.

Consider this scenario:

You have had a huge day at work, your boss has been on your back all day, and then you get home and the kids are playing up and your partner wants some attention. You feel stressed and anxious.

You feel like you 'need' a drink.

Why?

The fact that *most* of the anxiety you are feeling and the desire for alcohol is generated by the alcohol you consumed yesterday would be quite an 'inconvenient truth', wouldn't it?

How on earth would somebody who doesn't drink cope with this situation? Would they explode or at least burst into flames without the 'wonderful calming effect' of the alcohol?

Well, they *would* cope with it and they wouldn't need the alcohol, because they simply wouldn't be craving it in the first place.

In nature, every situation seeks balance and equilibrium. Alcohol is a depressant and exerts an effect on the brain. The brain then responds to try and restore balance. What is the opposite of depression? Stimulation. In this scenario, this stimulation manifests itself as *anxiety*. As you push down one side of this emotional 'seesaw' the brain pushes back to level it up and restore equilibrium. Over time, if there is no further stimulation or depression, the brain returns to a normal state once more. This is the domain of the non-drinker. Over time, the craving for alcohol kicks in and you can see where this is heading.

The non-drinker would, of course, feel some stress in the above scenario, but the stress would be **without** the anxiety caused by the alcohol craving. They would also not have to suffer the self-esteem-shattering feeling of NOT being able to cope without alcohol, and thus would be more able to deal with the situation in front of them.

Please read that paragraph again, and as many times as you need to in order to get past your own scepticism. This is your subconscious mind's greatest weapon, along with complacency and apathy. This is cognitive dissonance in action, so keep an open mind about what I am going to tell you, as it is going to change your life for the better.

Let's take the scenario above once more and amplify it even more – imagine a heroin addict faced with the same situation. They would be in acute withdrawal and highly agitated. How easily would they cope with the situation? Clearly not very well. It is exactly the same for alcohol, it's just the overall magnitude of the craving/satisfaction cycle is more subtle, so we don't associate the craving with the drug.

In my own experience, I had been drinking regularly and quite heavily since my mid-teens so that cycle of 'satisfaction' and then the resultant craving had been reinforced many thousands of times and my brain had simply come to accept it as the norm. *Not for one moment*, did I ever think that my general anxiety was down to the alcohol. I assumed (cognitive dissonance again) that I was simply anxious, as the direct result of being a high-performing individual in a big job, with lots of responsibilities.

I had been duped – and believed the alcohol was surely the *antidote* to this, not the cause of it! Wasn't it?

Waking up to this was a big part of my realisation of the wool that had been pulled over my eyes. Wool that had been knitted and double-stitched by peers, relatives, friends, TV, social conditioning and a desire to fit in for DECADES.

How this descent into dependence and addiction works:

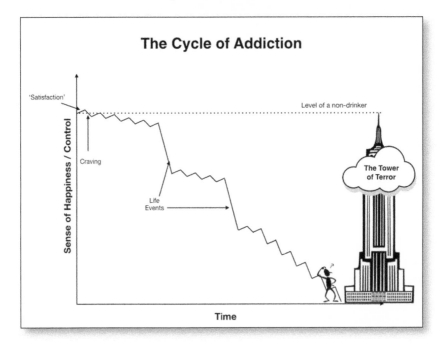

We have this cycle of 'satisfaction' and craving and over time our tolerance to alcohol increases.

As someone who would commit to 'Dry January' every year (mainly due to pressure from my partner, to be honest) afterwards I would always find that I would be able to get *extraordinarily* drunk on a mere fraction of the alcohol I was used to consuming. My body wasn't used to it, and the effect was fairly devastating. The hangover was colossal and my cognitive dissonance would tell me that the fact I felt so ill, was that I hadn't been consuming *enough* alcohol. Crazy!

The relentless downward trend this physical process creates can be extremely subtle. Periodically, something will happen and we 'let ourselves down' due to our excessive drinking, and we vow to get it under control. But we don't. The hangover is forgotten, the embarrassment we suffered fades into the past and we carry on like before, only worse. We need more of our addictive poison to achieve the same effect.

This process is relentless, but there will be moments when we are 'on our best behaviour' for a while and things feel on a more stable footing. Perhaps we have a new partner or a new job and the dynamic shifts. Over time, if the process itself isn't addressed, we end up back in the same place once more. When we get to a place of helplessness and we begin to really understand we are out of control, we feel worthless and isolated.

I have had many clients share pictures with me of opening a rarely used cupboard or drawer, to find empty bottles stashed in there from their drinking days. The guilt and shame too much to bear, meaning we hide the evidence – sometimes even from ourselves, as most of them don't even remember putting the bottles there!

From that place of helplessness, the way out seems virtually impossible. We have fallen so far from the person we were; we feel incapable of change. The debilitating fear, coupled with the self-esteem destroyed by alcohol, make the return to normality feel like an impossible task. Remember what I said about my emotions at the top of the Col d'Aubisque? That sense of achievement would have been absolutely impossible without a well-signposted route, a supportive crew and the camaraderie of my fellow riders.

There is a way out of this. You have to break it down into manageable chunks or the whole thing is so huge, so overwhelming and so unfamiliar, that to contemplate it will stop you from even beginning the process.

This is why I created the 'Tower of Terror', which we will deal with later in this book.

As depicted in the picture above, the Tower of Terror may be so tall that you cannot even see its summit. You don't know what the top floor is like, and you don't even know if you will like it when you get there. People may tell you the top floor is amazing, they may want you to experience it for yourself, but *unless you get going*, you will remain stuck in the lobby forever.

We will deal with this part of the journey – dealing with the fears we all experience – in a later chapter and by breaking them down into manageable chunks, the whole tower can be climbed.

Chapter Review:

Alcohol is a dangerously addictive drug that has become legitimised by society.

This perception is gradually changing in the same way it did for smoking, but there remains an enormous burden on a large section of society.

Some people have 'woken up' to this and are looking for answers. Others are not ready to accept their behaviour is damaging themselves and others.

This places you at the leading edge of this change, which can be occasionally uncomfortable or lonely, until you start to understand the benefits for yourself and your life begins to reshape itself in a better way.

Only then do the followers start to realise the folly of their behaviour.

Notes/Reflections

Chapter 3 – Exaggerations

In this next section, we will deal with exaggerations – all those 'myths' that are perpetuated from a whole variety of sources around us that build our own perception around alcohol.

Some of these myths come from the alcohol industry itself. Some of them come from society and society's pressures, because as humans – we *love* a myth, a legend, a *story*. We are relatively simple animals. If we hear the same piece of information from two or three different sources, we tend to accept it as the truth. Our subconscious mind is extremely open and extremely gullible!

Repetition is extremely powerful and I make no apology for saying the same thing in different ways throughout this book. Your subconscious is paying attention at all times, whether you like it or not! This is the one chapter where I'm *really* going to need you to try and put all your perceptions to one side. Keep an open mind and **really** examine your own perception with regards to some of these myths that we have around alcohol because a lot of these exaggerations are simply NOT TRUE. We have *accepted* them as being the truth, for a whole variety of different reasons, so it can feel difficult and quite challenging to have those reset because as human beings, we don't generally tend to like to do that.

If we are to change how we behave and how we feel, we need to challenge ourselves. You don't get a six-pack by continuing to sit on the sofa and eat pizza – you succeed by pushing your boundaries and 'comfort' levels.

Abs or Pizza – it's a choice.

Let me give you a couple of examples that you may want to consider before we get stuck into this.

It was only a few hundred years ago that we thought the earth was flat and everybody accepted that as being the truth. It took some very brave, intrepid explorers who were ridiculed at the time to actually prove that that wasn't the case. If those intrepid explorers had failed to return, for whatever reason, this would have at the time been accepted as PROOF that the world was flat and they had sailed off the edge.

Of course, we now all know that it is completely untrue. We've been in space – we've had a look at the planet from the moon, and we know *exactly* what shape it is. But a few hundred years ago, everybody believed that the earth was flat. Just before Roger Bannister ran the four-minute mile for the first time, a very eminent doctor wrote a paper actually PROVING that it was *impossible* for a human being to accomplish that feat.

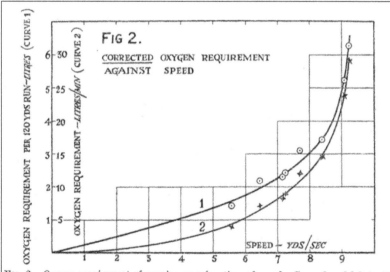

FIG. 2.—Oxygen requirement of running as a function of speed. Curve 1 and left-hand vertical scale, oxygen requirement per 120 yards run. Curve 2 and right-hand vertical scale, oxygen requirement per minute. The results shown have been corrected for the energy involved in "start" and "pull up" and represent the net requirement of running only.

Two months after he accomplished this, his biggest competitor, John Landy also ran under four minutes, narrowly losing to Bannister in the 1954 Commonwealth Games – with less training. Once a psychological barrier is broken, the progress is always rapid.

By way of another sporting example, Dick Fosbury, created the 'Fosbury flop', which is a now-familiar technique that we see in the high jump and was used, by him, in the 1968 Olympics. He brought that technique to the competition and it met with a very strong negative response, so typical of how we tend to react to things: What is our standard response when something challenges our sometimes long-held preconceptions?

You will go through these responses with some of the following:

The first one tends to be **disbelief** – 'What on earth was that? What did he just do?'

The second one might be to **ridicule** – to dismiss it and say, 'Well, it's frankly ridiculous, who would do such as a crazy thing?'

Then there may be an element of **denial** – 'Well, it's not fair! Clearly it's unethical to behave in such a way.'

Eventually we **accept** things for what they are, and we engage with them. They become part of our normal culture.

Great news – you're going to experience *all* of those things at some point as you read this, so an open mind is really important, if not vital, in order to progress. Be gentle with yourself – you are going to have similar reactions to some of the exaggerations that we're going to go through. But they are the truth, and they are the facts.

In order to move forward, you are going to have to incorporate them and accept them, but just be ready for those little reactions because your subconscious mind is not going to like it on quite a few different occasions, particularly the ones which you hold dearest, anyway! Remember the combination lock analogy? Get ready for some missing numbers!

Ready? Here we go.

Exaggeration #1 – 'Drinking helps me to relax'

Yep, let's get the big one out of the way. Life can be incredibly tough at times, and it's very tempting to say, '*Well, actually, you're the only thing I've got that actually makes me happy. It's my escape from all these things*'.

Let me start by asking you a question, which is the drink that makes you the happiest?

Is that the first drink?

Is it the second drink?

The tenth?

The last?

If you actually consider the fact that it takes alcohol around about ten minutes to exert an effect in the brain, that first drink has probably been consumed by the time you feel any effect from it *whatsoever*. So, any physical 'relaxation' has quite a delay.

By that time, we have moved on to the next one.

Whenever I am dealing with clients, one of the most often-asked questions, is 'What is wrong with me – why can't I just have the one?' and you are starting to understand the answer...

Alcohol affects everybody's judgment. There are drink-drive limits for everybody – not just the weak ones.

In the 1960s and 1970s, drink-driving was rife. The cognitive dissonance approach was to assume that 'only the stupid ones get caught' and 'I can handle it because I am a man/woman/fat/thin/ son of an alcoholic/pregnant/bald/the youngest of my siblings/can handle my beer better than cousin Dave', etc.

In fact, all of this was completely untrue. Studies showed that your objectivity disappears after alcohol starts circulating in your blood. The only reason there is a 'limit' is because as a society we decided that a degree of impairment was acceptable. This also is changing. Legal blood alcohol limits are falling and the only reason they are not being brought to zero is that it would be impractical to enforce for a variety of reasons. I'm fairly willing to bet that if you were to watch somebody who has had a lot to drink and they're having their tenth, fifteenth or twentieth drink you would see that they're not enjoying those drinks *at all*.

There is very little pleasure in them whatsoever – it's a means to an end. They are on a conveyor belt that they have very little control over. In fact, there's *no happiness involved whatsoever*. (Of course, generally when we observe these situations, we ourselves are intoxicated so don't notice!) Robert Downey Jr, the famous Hollywood actor, whose battles with both drink and drugs are very well documented, is quoted as saying with regard to alcohol:

> *It's like I have a loaded gun in my mouth. And I like the taste of metal.*
>
> Robert Downey Jr.

So really consider this – where *is* the happiness from that alcohol?

Well, I will tell you – it is generated around the *anticipation* of it.

It's the craving that you feel, and the anticipation of that craving being satisfied, which can *only* be solved by the alcohol.

That is the cruel irony of this whole situation.

The alcohol sets up this *expectation* that there is going to be happiness. By the time you realise there is no happiness, you no longer have sufficient rationality to care. Actually, when you really think about it, the happiness does not come from the alcohol itself, because it *can't*.

Generally, alcohol is *associated with* relaxation, it does not *create* relaxation. Take the time to fully process and digest that. If I were to hand you a glass of ethanol – that industrial solvent that is the active ingredient that you are craving – it plays little or no role in your relaxation, but it may be that when you choose to consume it, you are doing other things to relax.

A lot of people will drink at a time when they may be spending time with family and friends in a relaxing situation. You might be on holiday or socialising.

It is not the alcohol that is creating the relaxation in fact, it is quite the reverse!

We know that alcohol is a depressant and the human body will always seek some kind of equilibrium. So, for every time you force a depression on it, which is often mistaken to be 'relaxation', your body will create a corresponding **anxiety**.

That anxiety will manifest itself **as a craving for more alcohol**. Some people (and I know I was guilty of this) often manage the alternative with caffeine – and caffeine is a stimulant.

When you are drinking alcohol a lot, and you're having a lot of the depression, from the alcohol, you then need to force-create the stimulation, which can come from coffee, or perhaps from energy drinks, which all have their own addictive cycle. I hope you are starting to see the craziness of this behaviour. I use the words 'cruel irony' as they are highly accurate. You get trapped in a vicious cycle. You are consuming large quantities of a depressant which then needs to be addressed with some form of reverse stimulation.

So, we use caffeine to try and push ourselves back up again.

Later on, the alcohol itself creates its own anxiety and we add the stress of the craving. Given that we have spent time jacking ourselves up with anxiety-creating substances, **is it any wonder we feel like we need a drink to 'relax'?**

It's MADNESS, and it is not what non-drinkers experience. This is just a physical response – the actual sense that the alcohol creates a relaxation is a complete and utter fallacy. Even though alcohol is a depressant, and it *will* create a short-term numbing effect, in the long run there is ZERO relaxation to be had from it.

However, as imperfect human beings, we're very good at creating the association of relaxing times and all the other experiences and sensations that go with them. We will, of course, seek to attribute the outcome to the Alcohol.

Bad news: alcohol does not relax you – it actually does quite the <u>reverse</u>.

Awareness of this fact can be really helpful, but it isn't the only answer. I hope reading this makes you feel a little cheated and angry. Mischievous corporations, and fellow addicts, have sold you a lie. You are now beginning to see the 'Emperor's New Clothes' for what they are.

Exaggeration #2 – 'It's just a habit'

We tend to use the terminology of 'habit' and 'addiction' quite interchangeably these days, but they are two very different things. A habit is something that you have *control* over. Let's say I bite my nails, or pick my nose. While they may be bad habits, I certainly wouldn't be *addicted* to them. When it came to my consumption of alcohol, I had very little control over that whatsoever.

I would visit the supermarket on the way home from work, to buy that evening's dinner and convince myself I was going to have a night off the booze.

I'm not going to drink tonight, I'm not going to drink tonight, I'm not going to drink tonight… I would remind myself over and over again.

Twenty minutes later, I would head back to my car with two bottles of wine and a bottle of gin clinking ominously in my trolley, wondering, *How the f*ck did that just happen?*

This lack of control over what we are doing is so terrifying, we actively choose to ignore it. This is a good time to tell you that one of the biggest benefits of ditching the booze is that you once more feel that you are back in control of your life – like the captain who has just recaptured his ship from evil pirates. Back at the helm, he can pilot his ship towards safer waters.

Yes, there were habitual elements to it, i.e. routine, situations, etc. but actually what I was dealing with was an *addiction*. Why? There was a craving there that could only be sated by the alcohol itself – *nothing* else would do.

Remember – a habit is something that you have that might be a routine, but it's something that you are definitely in control of. Conscious awareness brings a change of behaviour relatively easily. An addiction is something very different – don't get the two confused.

Your alcohol <u>addiction</u> is not a <u>habit</u>.

Exaggeration #3 – 'Alcohol gives me confidence/calms my nerves'

This can feel like quite a positive use of alcohol to many people.

Well, I use it – it gives me some confidence, it calms my nerves, and it makes me more able to perform.

Let's just think about that for a little while. Why, particularly in social situations, which are generally what we tend to be talking about, do we get nervous? Why do we feel that bit of social anxiety? Why do we *want* to feel more confident?

In general, people feel nervous because they don't want to make a fool of themselves, or they don't want to appear stupid. They want to do the right thing and that's commendable and an innate desire that we all have. When was the last time, that you encountered a drunk person, where you felt that that was *actually* what was happening?

If you're sober, and thus able to see the truth of the situation and you encounter somebody who's been drinking a lot, they generally tend to be repetitive, irrational, emotional, long-winded or often a bit *boring*. They may have lost their sense around what's appropriate and can be over-familiar. Some people may be quite intimidating as they have lost their own 'radar' around the subtleties of non-verbal communication, and they can easily become aggressive and violent. Is that what they set out to achieve when they started 'drinking for confidence'?

Most heavy drinkers will have had those excruciatingly embarrassing reminders of the people who they insulted, the exes they drunkenly texted with inappropriate sentiments or the fact they simply made a fool of themselves. And so, the notion that the alcohol has had some kind of beneficial effect is, really quite lost.

By trying to avoid looking foolish, you became the fool.

All the things that you were *most* concerned about actually come *true*. The alcohol did that – it had the opposite effect from that which was intended. And yet, if we are around drunk people, it is hastily explained away as 'the drink talking' because nobody wants to admit it!

How many times have you woken up and thought, *Oh, my goodness, I need to go and apologise to that person, because I've said the wrong thing?* Or even just woken up with that nagging doubt and dread following a blackout. This actual notion that alcohol somehow gives you a constructive means of communicating with people and being confident is, frankly, bizarre.

Here is a quote from a lovely friend of mine from social media:

 ★ Rising star · 16 mins

Something incredible happened last night. I went to an audition for a big play in Nottingham and usually I would be drunk before I even got there. Stone cold sober and I was asked to read for the main part and got the job! I always thought I was a better actress with a good few drinks inside me but doing it sober was liberating and I brought so much emotion to the scene as my emotions all came through. Day 17 and feeling hopeful xx

 You and 26 others   7 comments

You are better than you think you are. What is the only force in your life that doesn't agree? Alcohol.

We choose to interpret the *numbing depression that alcohol brings* as 'calming your nerves' and 'giving you more confidence'. But when you look at it objectively, it's clearly not the case.

Exaggeration #4 – 'I like the taste of it'

Alcohol in itself does not taste nice. If I was to give you a glass of neat ethanol and you would have even a small sip of it, it would taste vile, make your eyes water, you would choke and you would cough. This is an industrial solvent, and it's a poison.

If you are in an accident and are taken to hospital with injuries, they will swab your wounds with alcohol. Would they do this to make your wound feel a bit happier after a traumatic experience? To calm your bleeding leg? To give it more confidence to begin the healing process? Of course not – the doctors or nurses will swab your wound with alcohol because it KILLS EVERYTHING that might infect you.

If I challenged you to drink a half pint of neat alcohol it would likely kill you. The entire drinks industry has had to try to come up with ever increasingly devious ways to make something that is **totally unacceptable** to the human palate, more acceptable, so you will consume it. They know if they do that successfully, the addictive nature will take over and you're hooked.

I used to be partial to whisky. The whisky industry plays with flavours by putting their ethanol into different casks, to try and imbue some kind of other taste, as well as watering it down to a level where it kills you slowly, rather than quickly. It's no accident that the industry has come up with 'alcopops'.

These 'lifestyle drinks' have got a lot of flavouring added to them to try and make something that is utterly unacceptable, acceptable. They go out of their way to mask the product they are REALLY selling in a way that distracts you from what you are really drinking. This exaggeration can be a difficult one to get past, I know.

I used to drink *industrial* levels of gin and tonic. Now I tend to drink tonic waters of various different flavours with some lemon and some ice. Guess what? I can't even tell the difference any more. The alcohol industry's 'secret weapon' – their ability to disguise their product – is their downfall for me.

Here is the 'inconvenient truth' for them – *a gin and tonic doesn't taste much different to a tonic on its own!* I don't necessarily advise simple substitution to alcohol free equivalents of what you have been drinking as a strategy because I believe it's not constructive and actually really short-sighted. You are also not tackling the emotional component of your drinking, whether it be a 'reward', 'relaxation' or whatever.

Here's another uncomfortable truth – alcohol makes you extremely **lazy** in a number of ways, one of which is that <u>you never try anything new!</u> Some people go straight from their favourite tipple to an alcohol-free version of it and then expect miracles to happen. If that is what it takes to get you sober then fine, but you need to hear me out on this:

You are depriving yourself of a world of new tastes and sensations by simply sticking to a different formulation of what you have been drinking.

Personally, I do not like the taste of alcohol-free beverages whatsoever.

Alcohol tastes awful but we want to like it and switching to an alcohol-free version of what got you into this mess doesn't make a lot of sense. It tells your subconscious that it is still OK to want this. This is your quest for your own personal answers. This is your 'combination lock'. Do not deprive yourself of a missing number by not exploring this issue.

Take smoking as an example:

You see people 'vaping' and feeling proud that they are 'not' smoking, while they billow clouds of nicotine – infused steam into your face.

While people tell themselves that they are stopping 'smoking' they are not tackling the nicotine craving, nor are they dealing with the psychological associations.

They continue to spend their hard – earned cash on these expensive newer products and now the data is starting to emerge that vaping has *serious* health consequences. These were not immediately apparent. If, as is likely, this trend progresses and that vaping nicotine is also harmful, they are no further forward – they have simply switched their addiction and associations to something else.

As I have mentioned before, this is a personal quest for your own answers. I read a 'Top tips for quitting drinking' article some time ago, and one of the so-called helpful suggestions was '*Try drinking soft drinks – you might like them'*. Saying this to an alcohol addict is pretty pointless, I am sure you can agree. It is like saying to a gambling addict – '*When the fun stops, stop'*. If you are addicted to gambling, the fun stopped a LONG time ago.

Near where I live there is a branch of a popular gambling establishment – a 'bookies' as we would call it in the UK. It is at the end of a row of shops that I visit regularly. Outside this establishment, there is an old tatty mountain bike leaning against the window most days. It is the sort of bike that would be bought for a minimal amount from a guy in a pub.

> Every time I see it, it epitomises gambling addiction for me. Whoever owns it is in there gambling *all the time*. They cannot afford a decent bike, let alone a car, and given that it is there during the day, I think it is not too big a leap to assume its owner is not in employment. The bike isn't even locked – the owner simply doesn't care if it is stolen as no discerning thief would bother with it. The next time you see an ad on the TV for a gambling company and you see how they portray their customers 'enjoying the thrill' of gambling, take some time to consider the reality and who they are *really* making their profits from.

So, while there is some 'truth' in this, it really only makes sense after you have found a way to get on top of the addiction first. Simply switching to a soft drink will not be a helpful suggestion, but when you feel strong, the search for new tastes and experiences you have denied yourself for years is *absolutely* part of this journey.

I drank pure water for quite a long time after quitting – purely and simply because I wanted to start from a completely neutral standpoint. I wanted something which was very bland and which I knew would do me good. It would get me hydrated, flush the toxins out and maximise my healing from the poison.

Over time, I began to crave tastes and started to experiment – thinking carefully about what I was 'missing' and looking for alternatives.

I mentioned I was a whisky drinker and I always drank it neat as I enjoyed the 'fiery' sensation. I discovered that ginger and apples when juiced into 'shots' gave me a similar experience and were extraordinarily good for me – packed with vitamins and minerals, whereas my 'old' choice was slowly killing me. I am not a big fan of fizzy drinks and sodas but that is a personal preference.

It would be unhelpful for me to say, 'drink this instead', but I am well within my rights to insist you go out, be curious, and find what works for you.

There is still the notion that alcohol tastes nice. If you think about a child having their first alcoholic drink, perhaps at a dinner party with the adults egging them on, they *want* to like it, even when they *don't* actually like it. They do so because they see all the grown-ups doing it. They *want* to like it so they will tolerate it.

Let's be clear, your first drink was *not* something that you enjoyed, no matter what you told yourself.

> **ALCOHOL may temporarily numb the pain, but it will make things much, much worse.**
>
> **SOBRIETY may temporarily be uncomfortable, but it will ultimately make things much, much better.**

Exaggeration #5 – 'A little alcohol is actually good for me'

This is a great one. Actually, there is some clinical data showing a marginal benefit of alcohol on certain clinical health markers. My background is in healthcare and I am used to running a critical eye over clinical studies and what they say and, more importantly, what they DON'T say.

There *are* some studies out there that show that a very low alcohol intake such as a maximum of one to three small drinks a day can have a tiny positive effect on things like blood cholesterol, which is a cardiovascular risk marker.

Now, let's be really, *really* clear that as a society, we are *desperate* for evidence that alcohol is not harmful. Bad news – the overwhelming evidence is that *any* amount of alcohol is dangerous. When your liver metabolises and breaks down alcohol it creates a carcinogen, acetaldehyde, which is proven to cause cancer in human beings. It also raises your blood pressure so any benefit on cholesterol is at least nullified. There will be some data that people will certainly cling on to and try to say it's not harmful. Our media is also complicit in this.

'Alcohol kills' does NOT sell newspapers. Maybe something like 'Stopping drinking causes Alzheimer's!' would be a better cover story? You do the math.

Let's be clear, if you are reading this book for the reason I think you are, then this whole section is completely moot as we are drinking *way beyond* anything that could even be tenuously construed to have a benefit! You know that you're really harming your health, but are desperate to try and feel better about your behaviour. Remember cognitive dissonance? This is exactly how it works. That is OK – it's normal. But now you know different.

The media will always vigorously promote something which is a perceived reason to advocate alcohol and your subconscious mind will absorb this, as it is very gullible. If it is aware of the *slightest* shred of evidence that there is a non-harmful element to drinking, it will interpret that as a fact.

In fact, your subconscious mind is working overtime on your behalf, to make you feel better about slowly killing yourself, as that is what you are continually asking it to do.

There is always somebody who will say, 'Oh, well, my uncle Joe drank three bottles of whisky, smoked twenty cigarettes a day, and lived until he was ninety-five'. That may or may not be true.

Tell that to the people who are in their forties, waiting for a liver transplant. Women *in their late twenties* are now presenting with irreversible cirrhosis of the liver and looking for a transplant.

Unfortunately, because in our society, we are all caning the living daylights out of our livers, healthy ones are in increasingly short supply for transplants.

The graph below terrifies me every time I see it. It shows the major causes of death in the UK.

EVERYTHING is reducing apart from ONE factor.

While we invest heavily into heart disease, respiratory illness, cancer and diabetes, deaths from liver failure are skyrocketing – up 400 per cent since the 1970s.

Don't be fooled. This is a dangerous and addictive drug, and it's a big killer, as well as destroying the lives of countless others.

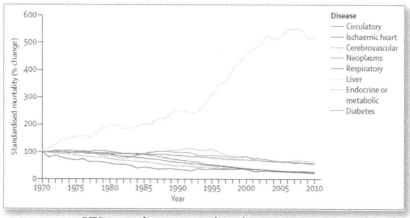

UK mortality rates indexed 1970–2010.

Alcohol does not do you the slightest bit of good in the overall scheme of things. Why does the media not tell us this information? Because it doesn't sell, and the incidence of alcohol addiction among journalists is even higher than the general population, so why would they?

Exaggeration #6 – 'Alcohol means you have a good time'

Human beings are social animals – we love to go out and be social with our friends. Society has created a scenario where that is often done on a Friday night in an establishment that sells alcohol. If you go into any town or city centre on a Friday or Saturday night, you will see what happens with people who've had far too much to drink.

You will see that very few people are really having a good time. You will see people becoming violent to people that they care about and being completely irrational. They are often disoriented and incapable of controlling themselves. You will see women who are vulnerable to any kind of attack because they are just unable to make good decisions or even physically protect themselves. A chief police constable of one of our big cities in the UK was interviewed about the prospect of legalising cannabis. (For the avoidance of doubt, I am not advocating substituting one addictive drug for another one!)

He stated that, as far as he was concerned <u>from a policing standpoint</u>, if they were to legalise cannabis and criminalise alcohol, he would be quite fine with that. His point was that when police are called to a situation where people are taking a different drug, there tends to be less trouble.

We have all been there – walking on eggshells around someone who is off their face with booze, being careful about what jokes you make in case they get offended. And yet we tend to interpret this as feeling like we are missing out.

Why do we feel this way? Our desire not to be the 'outlier' and to 'fit in' makes us want to conform, no matter how abhorrent or disgusting the behaviour is.

Tom Kerridge, the UK-based Michelin-starred chef who has been extremely honest about his battles with alcohol puts it like this:

I don't regret a single minute (of his drink-filled years). Every now and then I miss that guy. I miss the chaos… and I regret that I can't ever do that just once because I know that I can't be that person.

And this eloquently describes part of this journey. Tom speaks readily about how much his life has improved without alcohol. He lost a staggering 140 lbs when he quit the booze as he was a health time bomb.

I like his use of the word, 'chaos' – sometimes we all crave a bit of hedonism and to simply let loose, but we need to learn to understand the implications for us in doing that and it is a question only we can answer ourselves.

Robert Downey Jr. again:

I guess sometimes I want to have a drink with dinner. But then I remember that I have plans for Christmas.

So, while this is seductive and the social pressure that alcohol equals fun is not going to go away anytime soon, we need to be on our guard. We have seen what letting alcohol get its filthy claws into us can do, and we either choose to let it, or reject it.

Now this may feel a little downbeat and I intend it to be, as there is an ongoing threat of complacency. As we progress through this book, you will start to understand how to re-orient your life without alcohol at the middle of it, and that means alcohol has less and less of a place, in the same way as heroin or smoking has no place for someone who is not addicted to those drugs. The concept of 'fun' tends to change over the course of an evening. There's an interesting book that I read by Jason Vale, *The JuiceMaster* which said something that really struck with me.

Jason doesn't drink alcohol, so when out socialising with his friends, he mentioned there were three phases of the night:
'*I love you*',
'*I love you, you bastard*'.
And then just finally,
'*You Bastard*'.

I think that sums it up for me.

I go out to the pub with my buddies reasonably regularly. I really enjoy and engage with the early part of the evening. We catch up on news, everyone is making sense and, of course, tongues start to loosen and the laughter gets louder. I am now really good at spotting the 'tipping point' when people are getting inebriated and incoherent and the fun ebbs away pretty quickly.

Historically, I would have felt boring and lonely and would have consumed alcohol at breakneck speed to 'catch up' if I found myself in that situation. Now I simply leave them to it. Hugs are exchanged, knowing winks are given and off I go. Often someone will ask for a lift home at this stage, which I will happily do for them. After all, that is what friends are REALLY for, isn't it?

The following day, when they are nursing hangovers and kidding themselves about the 'great night' they had, I get the question, 'What time did you go?'
'About 10.30.'
'Oh, I didn't see you leave.'
'Yes, we said goodbye to each other and I gave Dave a lift back.'
'... oh... yes... I remember now...'
Who really had the better night? I caught up with everyone, remembered what they said, got to bed at a decent time, was a great friend to someone and woke up hydrated and full of energy. This thing I supposedly missed out on? Nobody can tell me what it was.

This is a shift in attitude, and you need to begin that process by challenging your own beliefs.

Exaggeration #7 – 'I have an addictive personality'

This is a really cruel trick that we play on ourselves, and it is a bit of a cop-out.

Actually, scratch that; it is a *total* cop-out. We're actually not taking responsibility for our own actions, because we're just saying, *'I've got no control over this'*.

In one respect that is true. We don't have conscious control over an unconscious behaviour. By telling ourselves we have some kind of defect, we allow our subconscious to gullibly accept this as the truth and thus it <u>never plays its part in helping us out of this.</u> The good news is that you DO have control over it. I appreciate that for some people, that's a bit uncomfortable.

There is no such thing as an addictive personality.

Although there may be some things in your life that have influenced you in terms of drinking or indeed other self-gratifying behaviours. Let me give you an example.

Imagine two identical twins who had an 'alcoholic' father.

Both of them are genetically *exactly* the same. One of them becomes a complete alcohol addict, because they may say, 'Well, that was the role model that my father was. So, I really had no control over it – what else was going to happen?'

Then you could have the other twin, who would say, 'Well, I've never touched a drink in my life because I saw my father completely addicted to this stuff. I saw the way he treated my mother; I saw the way that he treated us and swore that I would never ever, go down that same path".

65

The diversion point of these two paths could be so imperceptible that at the time, it would feel almost inconsequential. A chance happening. One twin seeing something that the other didn't. Over time, both twins develop attachment to their own viewpoint and the paths diverge. Neither twin knows what made them different, even though they are physically identical.

So, if there were such a thing as an addictive personality, or some kind of a genetic predisposition to this, then perhaps you could explain the incidence of smoking to me. What we've seen is that many years ago, around the time of the Second World War, soldiers were even *paid* in cigarettes, as part of their remuneration. As a result of this kind of thinking, around eighty per cent of males in the 1960s and 1970s were regular smokers.

Now, in the twenty-first century, this has plummeted to between fifteen and twenty per cent. What's different? Education.

If you go back fifty years, we thought that smoking wasn't bad for us. Now all the evidence to the contrary is available and it really is the truth. Through *education,* people have chosen to give up. Now smokers are very much in the minority. So where is the genetic element that kicked in within the last hundred years, and has now disappeared? That is just not how human beings evolved. It just doesn't happen that fast.

So, this whole concept of some kind of physical predisposition is very convenient for some people. But unfortunately, there is no science in it whatsoever.

THIS IS GOOD NEWS! There is not some genetic force within you that is going to prevent you from being successful. This simply means that it is within your control and through following some very clear and very obvious steps, you can make the changes that you need and there is nothing actually holding you back.

Perhaps you find some of your same behaviours manifesting themselves in other ways. Maybe you gamble, or you're addicted to porn, sex or coffee.

It's all born out of the same thing – a misguided association that you can get some kind of relief for whatever you're trying to escape from. Any one of these can easily create an addictive response in the brain.

As I've said before many times, **these cravings are only ever satisfied by the things that created them.**

You can see how the cycle will get perpetuated time and time again. Great news though – there is no physical 'thing' that's stopping you giving up alcohol whatsoever.

Exaggeration #8 – 'Giving up is alcohol is hard and requires sacrifice'

A real concern for many people that is perpetuated through every single branch of the media is that there is this huge sacrifice that has to be made. If I could just look you in the eye and tell you that the *complete reverse is true* that there is no sacrifice to be made and that there are ONLY benefits that will come out of the positive decision that you're making, I **would**. Unfortunately, I can't simply tell you that – you need to work this out for yourself.

We are conditioned into thinking that this is some kind of massive journey that you have to go on and that it's miserable. Coming up in the next chapter I will be talking about the 'Tower of Terror'. This tower is my interpretation of how we perceive the gap between what we *think* the reality is going to be, and what the reality *actually* is. At the beginning, it feels completely insurmountable.

What you will see as we go through the programme is that with just a little bit of guidance, this is not an insurmountable difficulty at all. When I went to hypnotherapy, I had a desire to fix whatever was broken in me. I was convinced that I was in some way faulty as a human being. I just wanted to go to sleep and wake up with someone having fixed me. That didn't work for me. That's not to say that it wouldn't work for you. My experience of hypnotherapy was that it was a relaxing thing to do. It simply didn't change my attitude in the long run to alcohol whatsoever.

I had a huge desire to be fixed by something external. It was a bit like going to the doctor in pain, like I used to when I was afflicted by gout. I just wanted the pain to go away. Give me a tablet, a pill, so I don't have to face the fact that I may have in some way brought this on myself. For the record people who don't drink at all can still get gout, but for me this was absolutely alcohol-driven.

But there is no magic pill for this.

Because the real solution is BETTER.

If I were to say to you, 'I can put you to sleep, and wake you up in three months. You will wake up and you will feel better in just about every aspect of your life. Tensions would be eased at work and at home. You would have more money in your pocket, you would be sleeping better, you would be feeling more positive, your physical health would have improved, and your self-esteem would have returned. You just have to swallow this magic pill'.

You would take that pill, wouldn't you? Of course you would. Just take a moment to imagine that feeling of waking up, three months from now, with little or no desire to drink. All cravings gone. Completely clear of this misery that got you reading this book. I mean, you'd be crazy not to take the pill, right?

Now imagine I said that there was a bit of a good news/bad news thing going on. We had run out of the pills.

'Oh no!', I hear you cry. 'This is just typical of my luck!' you may say and you would start to feel pretty despondent that a 'better life in three months' was rudely snatched from your grasp. Curses!

But great news! The pill was purely a memory suppressant, designed so that you would not remember the journey you undertook to achieve your goals.

All the tools, all the lessons were still there. The only difference is that you would remember the process, but thankfully there is nothing arduous or painful about it. In fact, the reason we had run out of the magic pills is that we realised we simply didn't need them in the first place.

In fact, the reason there are no pills left is that we stopped making them because people didn't want them. They learned so much about themselves in those three months, that they *wanted* to remember.

So, this does require some effort. There never was, or will be, a magic pill.

You have to **read the book, reflect on the learning** and **engage in the online content.**

But that is it. There are no marathons to run, mountains to climb or oceans to swim. Simply follow the process and take note of the little 'shifts' as they occur.

These are your missing numbers in your combination lock. You have to do this inner work, internalise things and accept the learning.

In fact, I am not really asking you to DO anything. What I am asking at your request is for you to STOP doing something. Something that causes you pain, misery, guilt, shame, embarrassment and low self-esteem.

At university, I studied physics. Any change of momentum in any direction, requires effort – it requires a force to be applied but you are doing that so just trust the process. You will get there. It is inevitable, if you take responsibility for finding the solutions inside yourself.

What I found personally was that while I did this inner work, there were some benefits that are immediate. I felt excited, hopeful and optimistic – perhaps for the first time in years. Actually, applying yourself to this is its own reward!

Some benefits can take time to come. My wish for you is that you follow the process, and you get to a situation that feels a bit like, 'Yeah, I can do this'.

And then your confidence builds. And builds. And builds some more. And keeps on building. Each little 'aha' moment builds upon the last one and you get this unstoppable feeling and it is amazing. Then at some point, you take a moment to look back and say,

'What on Earth was I thinking – it really wasn't that hard.'

This is *your* journey. You are part of the way along that journey. You're not there yet. But you've also come a long, long way. So, congratulate yourself for that.

I was reading a book on addiction. The way the author described this journey really resonated with me. He said it's a bit like you're in prison. The key unfortunately is in your pocket, and you are the jailer. For every move you make, you will also make the counter move, because your subconscious mind knows you inside out and wants to preserve the status quo.

This is why you do need some help from an external party, you can't really do this on your own.

I had to solve this alone because I couldn't find anybody to help. My whole rationale of doing this is to ensure you don't have to go through a decade of trial and error, procrastination, pain and failure. I would save you that level of time and money investment. I probably spent around £50,000 and saw a marriage disappear in that time.

If I can, and if you will let me help you by following in my footsteps, I can save you from that.

Exaggeration #10 – 'Not drinking makes you boring'

I used to love watching the TV programme *Friends*. I think probably everybody has seen at least *one* episode of it. There was one very interesting episode, which had a huge lasting impact on me, and I really only realise that now.

It was the episode called 'The One With Russ'. This episode introduces a character called 'Fun Bobby' and Fun Bobby is one of those popular extra characters brought into the season for a couple of episodes. He was Monica's boyfriend, and all the characters *loved* Fun Bobby – he was really popular.

Finally, they realised the reason why Fun Bobby was 'fun' – it was because he drank way too much. The cast regulars challenged him about it and told him his drinking was a problem. And so, he stopped drinking. And he became completely *boring*. So, everyone starts saying, 'Fun Bobby's not fun anymore' and instantly falls out of love with him.

To make matters worse, in order to cope with the fact that her boyfriend has gone from being 'fun' to 'boring' Monica begins to drink excessively. Bobby ends up finishing the relationship saying to Monica, *'I am not ready to be in a co-dependent relationship right now. And by the way, I think you need to get some help, because you drink too much!'*

Sometimes people write to me and say they aren't sure how or why they got into such a bad place with their drinking, and **this is often why**. It's not because you are weak, but because this kind of subtle message is **everywhere**. And your subconscious laps it up *without question*.

Now I look back and I realise it had quite a lasting impact on me. It was my favourite TV show and I had completely bought into the whole thing. Actually, I would like to believe that the reverse is true – not drinking makes you the fun one!

When I am not slurring my words and being the drunkest person in the room, I'm a far more interesting character and I am much more conversational.

I listen to people. And I actually remember what they say to me. So, what is boring about that?

If you arrive late to a party, and you've not had a drink, everyone else may be quite drunk. Are all those people the most exciting and fun people that you've ever met? No, they're not because they're generally plastered. They're not in *any* way fun, engaging and the life and soul of the party, no matter how loud and brash they are. In the past, I would arrive at a party like that and think, *I need to go and drink quickly to catch up*.

When you think about it, that's just crazy, because we just cannot bear the fact that everybody else is being a fool. The easiest way for us to cope is just simply to join them. When you actually see it for what it is, joining in is simply unhelpful to anyone, because drunk people tend to be loud, overbearing, boring, repetitive, as I've said before. And yet this old myth is relentlessly perpetuated through the media that people who don't drink are not fun. Once the wool is pulled from your eyes, often the reverse is true.

Exaggeration #11 – 'You can just cut down'

I personally empathise with this one a lot. When I got started on this path, it was absolutely *not* my intention to stop drinking altogether. I just wanted to be in control, because I knew I was completely *out of control*. For me, 'control' was being able to take it or leave it. Actually, looking back on this, it was really 'leave it' as the 'take it' part was going just fine!

As you go through this book, you'll be starting to understand the nature of addiction, and the fact that alcohol is a highly addictive substance, which is not widely acknowledged. We accept that heroin, nicotine, cocaine and other drugs are addictive, but accepting alcohol is the same is way too inconvenient for society. So whatever control looks like for you is up to you. It is simply not my job to tell you to do one thing or another with regard to your drinking.

I am not going to prescribe, and say that *'You shouldn't cut down'*, that *'You have to give up'*.

What I AM going to insist on however is that you give yourself a **break.**

Because only by taking a break do you get that control, whatever that looks like for you in the longer term.

Read those last two lines again. And again, until you learn I am *deadly* serious about this.

If you wanted to get fit and lose weight, you would eat better and exercise more. Simply joining a gym, watching the money leave your bank account and then going and sitting in the jacuzzi is not going to get a six-pack. You have to go and put yourself into a position of discomfort. Only then do you begin to grow and adapt.

And this is no different. If you decide to 'reward' yourself with two bottles of red wine on a Saturday night, you never get to face down why you see alcohol as a reward. Or find other ways to reward yourself. Alcohol makes you *lazy* and stops you finding new behaviours that are more constructive.

So, take a break, work out all your answers, and then all options are open to you. In certain circumstances I would have a sip of champagne, if somebody is celebrating and there was nothing else because I would like to honour whatever it was that they are celebrating. I simply can't be bothered to muddy the waters by trying to have to explain to people why I just want a soft drink. If somebody's celebrating something, it's not about me – it's about them. This is probably born out of a personal desire to fit in if I'm being brutally honest. I am not advocating this as an approach for you, and I watch myself like a hawk if I do. One sip. That's it.

Cutting down when you're on that addictive cycle absolutely does not work. All you do is take two steps up the escalator that you're on. But the escalator is still going. As you go through this book, you will begin to realise exactly what alcohol is, and what it isn't. As you are reading this, there is that little voice that you have inside your head, saying, 'You're better than this.'

Right now it's a whisper. It is a bit like a small child tugging at the tail of your coat. I'm giving it a f*cking megaphone!

You *know* all this stuff.

You know it's bad for you.

You know it's not helping.

Together we are building 'the case against' to get some balance back and to actually explode some of the truths that the old beliefs were built on. Cutting down is one of them, but it doesn't work. I see so many people saying, 'I cut down and ended up worse than before' or 'I tried to moderate and found I couldn't'.

Where is the fun in moderation anyway? It is a frankly ridiculous 'halfway house' state of affairs that achieves nothing and is actually harder than not drinking in the first place. The planning that is required for moderation of alcohol is *immense*. Don't do that to yourself. Take a clean break, whatever your goals are for the future. Whatever you do after this break is genuinely up to you. I believe that when you finish this book, you may make a different decision.

You may say, 'Okay, I see this for what it is, now'.

If I were a heroin addict and you never had used that drug before and I said, 'You have got to try this, it's awesome,' you wouldn't – because you would understand what the implications would be. If you are a non-smoker, and somebody offers you a cigarette, you would simply say 'No, I don't smoke' and that would be it. You don't *need* to smoke, and you probably also understand that smoking does not improve your life in any way, shape, or form.

The same is also true for alcohol. We are all buried so deeply into the conspiracy, we have lost sight of that. A smoker would describe in great detail as they lit up a cigarette how those wonderful moments of relaxation are the best parts of their day. They may say how they couldn't survive without them, and how they crave those moments when they are not there.

They are not lying. Those moments are very important to them. The big irony is that non-smokers also experience those moments. They just don't have a cigarette between their lips.

As there is a social stigma, there are other social pressures that go with it, so we do have a desire to just 'cut down' so we don't have to face the prospect of changing our perceptions.

So, if you are this far through the book, please make a deal with me.

Give yourself 100 days off alcohol. That way you can objectively assess what is going on. You can work out whether it's right for you.

If this feels a little scary and you have been to https://soberinseven. com/bookresources, then you can purchase the 100-day follow up email programme which will get you through it, provide inspiration and motivation and also give you some real structure around your journey back to happiness.

Why *would* you want to go back to something that disorients you, that is toxic, kills your liver, kills your brain cells, damages your nervous system, creates stress on a daily basis, creates anxiety and that creates cravings. You wouldn't want to go back to that.

In fact, the number one question that I get from people whom I know is, *'Are you still not drinking?'*
I may have told them two or three times that I've given it up and I'm not going to drink again, and yet they still can't quite believe it. So just be ready for that kind of pressure. It messes with people's heads a little bit. Over time, you start to get to like that a bit, because it makes you different and people will want to know your secret.

'First, they ask you why you do it, then they ask you how you did it.'

Virtually ALL regular drinkers are addicted. It is how this substance works. The strong ones like you have woken up to that fact but many are still trapped.

See the following social media post from a member of one of the big 'sober groups'.

1 hr ·

So I'm sat at Brighton train station after a massive fight with my best friend in the whole world. In my defence he was a complete dick, said I was exactly like my dad (dad is a recovering alcoholic). but it doesn't excuse the fact that if I hadn't drunk last night it would have been handled better and I probably wouldn't be here. You were all fucking right, moderation is a crock of shit. As is my so called friend. Day 1

9   7 Comments

Unfortunately, this is what moderation looks like in most instances. You are setting yourself up for a lifelong battle against your own physiology and psychology and it is little better than uncontrolled addiction itself.

If you want to spend the rest of your life doing the equivalent of riding a bucking bronco, then 'moderation' is for you!

Exaggeration #12 – 'I can take it or leave it'

So, if your goal is to 'take it or leave it', then why not 'leave it'?

(In the video programme, I pose this question, eyeball you directly down the camera lens and pause for dramatic effect.)

Serious question, though: **Why. Not. Just. Leave. It?**

Because you *can't*.
And that is OK – don't worry – we are doing something about that, you and I.

Consider the effect of the smoking bans that are now in place in many countries. Many smokers would not have seen themselves as addicted before these bans came into force. All of a sudden, they were stuck outside in the pouring rain, maybe alone, puffing away and all their friends were inside in the warm. They needed to satisfy their addiction and whereas they had told themselves they smoked 'to be social', they now were generally *not* having a great time and were isolated. For the first time many woke up to the fact that they actually had an addiction.

Many people *did* stop smoking, (the stats are remarkable) but many people just realised once and for all that they couldn't simply 'take it or leave it' and they did need to have their 'fix'.

Alcohol is an addictive substance and it is <u>exactly the same situation.</u>
If an alcohol ban came in tomorrow, you would suffer exactly the same fate.

During Prohibition in the US, illicit alcohol was the most lucrative black-market trade and that's because people needed to satisfy that addiction. Because they couldn't 'take it or leave it' prohibition didn't work. There was always a market for criminal gangs to exploit and over time the lawlessness created its own pressure as prohibition clearly was not the answer.

Ironically commercial pressures were also a factor as governments realised there was money to be made from alcohol taxation when the Great Depression took hold in 1929. Prohibition lasted a little over a decade.

Interestingly, during the time of prohibition, liver cirrhosis rates, infant mortality and alcoholic psychosis plummeted, despite the fact the law was widely flouted.

Exaggeration #13 – 'Alcohol gets me through tough times'

I hope by now you are starting to get the picture that alcohol does not help you through *any* tough time.

Financial problems? Alcohol *'helps'* you by costing you money. Lots of it. I spent £50,000 on alcohol in a decade. What kind of financially different situation could I have been in without that expenditure? I was lucky in that I had well-paying jobs, but this is the equivalent of me working at least a year of my life, to support the profits of the big alcohol companies. What a mug! In addition, it actually robs you of the time and energy you need to do something about whatever you are facing.

Relationship problems? Alcohol is *only ever* going to make that worse. When you are trying to repair relationships, lowered inhibitions, a loose tongue and the paranoia inherent in alcohol addiction are the last things you need.

Problems with your career? How can you *possibly* have the energy to do anything about that, if you are feeling below par every morning? It might be that you've got a dream of starting your own business. If you had a couple of hours each evening to devote to that, you could probably make something happen. If you're already on the wrong side of a bottle of wine, then that's just never going to happen.

The thing we tell ourselves that gets us through the tough times simply perpetuates them. It's a bit like just kicking a can down the road all the time, there's a little bit of gratification from kicking the can, but you just keep kicking it out of reach.

That can represents your future – *your* dreams, *your* aspirations and you keep kicking it out of reach. Alcohol does not help one little bit. And you know this is true.

Exaggeration # 14 – 'Not drinking means I will miss out'

Let me present a list to you of the things you *gain* by putting alcohol in its proper place. The 'counter argument' if you will.

You are getting more time. You are going to discover you have loads more useful time, whether it's in the evening or more productive time in the morning. However you choose to fill that is up to you, but by having a sense of your goals, dreams and aspirations of the life you want, you can now start taking steps towards them.

You'll have more money. I was spending (from my net income) £5,000 a year on booze. The day I stopped, I got a near £10,000 pay rise.

How hard would you work for a £10,000 pay rise?

What would you spend this on? Holidays, treats, investments – whatever you would prioritise as important to you are now no longer an indulgence – *you earned them* through your sobriety.

You'll have better mental health. Alcohol is a depressant. When you stop depressing yourself, it will come as no surprise that you will feel lighter, more positive, more resourceful and optimistic.

You'll have better physical health and appearance. The first few days can feel a bit bumpy, but when your body resets, your skin clears and your eyes brighten. You begin to look 'better' and the compliments begin. 'Younger' and 'healthy' were regulars for me and also 'thinner' even though I didn't lose tons of weight until I started exercising properly. The fact my bloated, blotchy face calmed down made it look like I had slimmed down immensely.

You will have better sleep. Perhaps not for the first few nights as your body detoxes, but after a couple of weeks you will really begin to notice the quality of your sleep begin to improve.

You'll have better focus to achieve whatever your goals are and you will be better equipped to do something about them.

You will have more energy. Alcohol kills your energy levels and the sad thing is you have probably forgotten what having energy actually feels like! You will be so used to operating at, say, seventy per cent of your optimum so that when your energy levels begin to climb it feels simply amazing.

There are many reasons for this, but a key one is that alcohol causes your red blood cells to bloat and become sticky. Your blood is thicker and less oxygenated. These cells replace every three months. This is why people report a drop in blood pressure and also resting heart rate – a marker of cardiovascular health. (Need any more reasons for three months off?) Better red blood cells = more oxygen = less stress on your heart = more energy. Your chances of a stroke, heart attack and certain cancers also drop significantly.

You'll have better self-esteem. You no longer have the '*What did I say*' paranoia, or have that self-loathing that goes with feeling that you're not in control of the situation with your alcohol cravings. This is one of the most under-reported 'benefits' of ditching alcohol and is hard to describe. As an old friend of mine might have said, '*It's a bit like trying to explain sex to a virgin*'!

You will have better relationships. It's well documented that alcohol is often one of the key reasons in a relationship breaking down, particularly when there is a discrepancy between what either party drinks.

You'll simply have a better <u>future.</u> Only you know just how much alcohol is costing you. How much alcohol is robbing you of your dreams and happiness. I don't need to labour the point, but just use this 'counter argument' to really fuel your fire on this. You will not snap your fingers and solve it in an instant, but if you have seen anything of my story, you will see how my life *began to* change beyond recognition the moment I took the alcohol hand-brake off.

So if I asked you if you're 'missing out on something', I think you'd be pretty hard pressed to come up with a better list than that in terms of what you fear that you might be missing out on, as opposed to the benefits of what you get back.

If you feel you need to, quantify this. Write down exactly what you fear you would be missing out on. I am willing to bet there is nothing on that list you have to actually miss out on without alcohol. Some adaptation of your thinking may be required and different expectations applied but you miss out on nothing by changing whether or not there is industrial solvent in the bottom of your glass.

I will probably 'rattle your cage' with quite a few of those. But please just take your time to digest what I have said. As you read that there will be some things you may have easily accepted. You simply go, 'Yeah, you're right' and some may take a bit of processing.

When I get feedback on these, invariably different people struggle with different ones. Some may be quite challenging for you but it is the truth of the situation. So, for each one that you struggle with, someone else has accepted that as the truth, because that is what it is – the truth. And vice versa. We are all different, with a different set of beliefs. We are unifying around some universal truths – allow yourself the opportunity to get there by digesting these.

Consider this:

Two football fans are sitting next to each other in a football stadium. As such they have a near-identical view of what is happening on the pitch.

The striker of one team breaks free, tears down the wing and a goal looks like a certainty. Only one defender stands between him and the goalkeeper. The striker is about to hit what is surely going to be the winning shot, when the defender tackles him, and he goes down in the penalty area.

'Penalty!!' cries one fan.

'What a tackle!' cries the other.

How can it be, that two people with near-identical viewpoints can have such differing interpretations of the event?

What is different about these two?

Simple. It is the colour of the scarf and shirt that they wear.

Our belief system is the filter through which we view the world. A lifetime of programming, prejudice and influence from those around us change our view of the truth in *every* situation. It is your job to unpick these beliefs as they are holding you back. Remember that natural human response we talked about before?

It tends to be disbelief, and then denial. You may seek to ridicule a little bit. This is your subconscious reacting, and also checking that you are serious about this new information. Give it any doubt, and the status quo will be resumed. Over time, as you consider these truths, your subconscious mind will accept them and your feelings begin to change.

By definition, this is a subconscious process. You will feel your acceptance shift, even though consciously it doesn't feel like a lot is happening.

Whenever you feel challenged, this is actually a sign that you're moving forward.

Don't be bashful about it – it is really great and part of this process! Take the time to absorb these before moving on.

Having your eyes opened to the truth can feel challenging, but think of the first time you saw High Definition TV, or even, if you are my age, the first time you saw colour TV. That TV that you spent so long watching in the past that you were totally happy with, now doesn't seem so great anymore, because you now can comprehend what 'better' looks like.

Chapter Review:

Which exaggerations/myths have been instrumental in supporting your addiction and keeping you stuck?

Do you really understand the truth of them now? If yes, how will you capitalise on this new-found awareness? If no, what further research do you need to do to fully understand the reality of the situation?

How was this process for you? Were you able to be curious and to keep an open mind, or was it difficult for you? Who can you chat to who will help you process this?

Notes/Reflections

Those who overcome addictions may be the strongest people on the planet.

DW

Linda's Story:

2013 was when things first got really bad.

I suffer from social anxiety and it seemed to happen around the playground. I'd given up work so I didn't feel I fitted in with the working mums, but I didn't gel with the stay-at-home group either. So, I started to drink before social occasions, not a lot at the beginning, just a 250ml glass of wine... but then it wore off and I would get shaky and need more and more.

I ended up going to my son's nursery show and being so drunk that I couldn't remember the ending.

I would wake up in the morning and need a drink just to get out of bed. I would have gulps of it, and then throw it back up, until I could get a bit into my system. It was disgusting, there was no enjoyment in it, I just couldn't actually function without it.

Someone smelled alcohol on my breath at nursery and called the police. They were actually very supportive but despite the shock of their visit, I still couldn't stop. First wine, then alcoholic ginger beer, then vodka. I was never a vodka drinker before. I mixed it with Lucozade as I was barely eating anything.

I looked a total mess, my eyes were yellow, my face was bloated. People asked me all the time whether I was ill. I was always drinking, never really drunk but always topping up.

Eventually doctors got involved and I ended up in rehab on a seven-day detox. They did a liver function test and mine was 3500, vs. a normal reading of 50 to70! I wasn't ever a '2 bottles of vodka' drinker, but my body clearly couldn't get it out of my system effectively. I was terrified.

It was a traumatic time, but I got back on track and within five months, my liver levels had returned to normal. I saw a clinical psychiatric nurse for a couple of years and was given medication to relax my muscles and take the edge off my anxiety.

Everything was OK for a while but by the end of 2017, my drinking was creeping back up. I was losing control but I'd made promises to family and friends the previous time, so I couldn't risk them finding out. I knew it was wrong, I hated myself for it, but I had dug myself into a hole with drink and now with the anxiety drugs too and I just couldn't get out.

I started drinking before picking my son up from school, brushing my teeth to hide it. Then, I'd have another couple of glasses before dinner, not from the bottle in the fridge, but from one I had hidden away. I stashed them in my son's wardrobe, in an old school bag. It was never masses (I never needed much to feel numb), but it was relentless.

I would wake up at 3 a.m. with palpitations, knowing I was sliding backwards.

I was depressed and couldn't muster up the energy to even wash my hair. My daughter found a bottle of wine hidden in her wardrobe and was devastated, but it was a fall that finally brought it to a head. I tripped leaving the hairdressers (ironically, I was sober at the time) and landed hard on my arm.

It puffed up and a nurse friend said I should get it looked at. But I was too scared to see a doctor in case they did another liver test. My whole arm went black so eventually I was forced to go to hospital, where I learned it was broken. I had to have an operation and was terrified my drinking would be found out and that I would be exposed. As it was, they didn't do any tests, but the absolute fear of being found out was horrific.

I knew I needed to find something else, some other way of getting help. I didn't want to go to groups, as I live in a tiny community and didn't want to risk bumping into someone I might know, like another mum from school.

I looked online for a private, anonymous way to sort myself out again and found the programme. The joy of it was that I didn't have to tell anyone. None of my family knew I was doing it and I went through the modules whenever I could – when everyone else was sleeping or out.

I loved the fact that it was seven days long and I became completely absorbed, immersed in it – I wasn't really thinking about anything else. The week-long duration was important as it kept up the momentum which I needed. I think I might have wandered off and had a drink if it had been more spread out.

I loved the videos and the 100-day emails were hugely important too: I really waited on them coming into my inbox, wondering, *What is it going to be today?* Also, even though it was an online programme, I didn't feel on my own, I knew if I wanted, I could email you and, having been through the process, you would understand. It no longer felt one-way.

I still look at the Tower of Terror now and I use it for dealing with other issues too, like conflict with my partner. It also helps me deal with the people who don't really like how I've changed for the better, 'Ooh you've lost weight, have you been ill?' That's a bit annoying, but the Tower gives me tools for dealing with others and their negativity.

One particular one thing that was powerful for me was the 'Future Self' Meditation. I can remember tears running down my face as I did it. It gave me real clarity and it came at just the right moment. I had really vivid pictures in my head of my two different futures and this exercise really helped me identify where I was going.

It has inspired me to throw myself into meditation. I do it every day now. And I do the breathing as well, so I have something to focus on when I'm out with other people and feel anxious. I've joined a meditation group – I would never have been able to do that when I was drinking, but leaving the alcohol behind is creating space for me to do the other stuff that is more life enhancing.

I think that the biggest thing is that I'm beginning to be the person I visualised in that future-self meditation. That is really amazing.

Physically, I look completely different. I've lost weight (I've now got definition on my stomach – I never thought that would happen!), I go to the gym and my liver tests are all normal. I take pride in my appearance, enjoy shopping now. And now I can look at myself and think I'm doing well. I've even been asked to take part in a photo shoot for work, which has been a huge confidence boost.

The biggest change for me though, is in how I feel better mentally. I no longer take the anti-anxiety drugs before going out, and the anxiety itself has dropped by 50–70%. I feel calmer and more relaxed and I no longer wake up worried in the night.

It's fair to say that sometimes I feel my emotions are a bit too strong, but maybe that's because I'm not numbing things now. There's still work to be done for sure, but I feel braver now and it's improving all the time. Plus, I feel motivated which I think is the big change – I'm pushing myself, and making myself do more social things.

I can remember a moment during the programme where I walked up a hill near my house. At the top is a bench, I sat there and felt amazing: full of relief, hope and happiness. It was the first time I had felt happy for such a long time – it was overflowing, I was bubbling with it.

I've not had a drink since doing your course. It's been amazing and it's changed my life. Thank you.

Chapter 4 – Endurance

Building endurance has a lot to do with facing fears. It is about keeping going, when the voices in your head cry 'stop'.

My Tour de France journey taught me this over and over again. I had read all the books, listened to the audios, but it wasn't until I rode the Tour that I finally got it.

On 12th July 2018, I rode the 'Queen Stage' of the Tour – a 130-mile monster of a day with an equivalent amount of climbing of nearly two-thirds of Mount Everest in a day. The sun rose in a clear blue sky over the mountains and conditions were perfect.

It was chilly as we dropped down the mountain from La Rosiere to start just after sunrise. As I was now a seemingly renowned downhiller, I pushed to the front and for the first (and only) time of those three weeks I actually led the entire field. The Col de Madeleine was enjoyably climbed and the eye-boggling Lacets de Montvernier despatched in good humour. My best buddies and I even paused to play like children in the fountain at the summit in the searing heat which remains one of my abiding memories. The bigger challenge of the Col de la Croix de Fer arrived just after lunch. A massive, brooding twenty-nine kilometre slog up a seemingly endless ribbon of tarmac snaking its way to an unseen summit.

Throughout my training, there were two mountains that really scared me. One was the Col du Tourmalet in the Pyrenees and the other was this one – the longest single climb of the entire race. It took me over three and a half hours to accomplish.

At the summit I was elated. I knew I had passed a significant milestone, and was actually feeling pretty good. I dropped down the mountain as the sun began to sink in the sky and I happily thrummed along the tarmac to the bottom of the iconic Alpe D'Huez. The finish for the day lay at the top, somewhere in the deepening gloom. As I approached the final water stop at the bottom of the 'Alpe' I posted this on Facebook:

What the picture doesn't show is the van and minibus that the support crew were using. On the tail lift of the van were six men who had given up for the day and who were waiting for a lift to the summit. As I walked up to grab a final banana or two and refill my water bottles, they were all studying me closely, as if wondering what I was going to do.

When I met their gazes, they were literally pleading with their eyes for me to join them, as it would have made them feel better about the decision they had taken. Then a very strange thing happened. My good feeling and confidence evaporated.

My excuses came like a Tsunami.

'It's late – getting up to the hotel at a reasonable time would be helpful.'
'You've done really well. Why not reward yourself?'
'It's going to be dark by the time you get up there. Will your lights hold out?'
'There's no shame in stopping – you have already had a huge day.'
'Your wrists are hurting – give them a rest.'
'The physios might have packed up by then and you could miss out on a massage.'
'Will there even be any food left by then?'

I was totally unprepared for it and I had a big 'wobble' mentally.
Yogi, the mechanic, seemed to sense my sudden indecision,
'You up for this, Andy?' he asked.

'Hell, yes!' I lied, at the very least trying to convince myself.

And then another strange thing happened. The *instant* I swung my leg over the crossbar, the feelings disappeared. I was ready, I was committed and I wanted to get going. Off I went, up the infamous twenty-one hairpin bends of the Alpe D'Huez.

An hour later, Yogi drew alongside me as I ground out the pedal strokes in the darkness. In the glow of my single bike light, I saw his face. He smiled warmly and gave me a gentle nod. Not one of the men in the back of the minibus met my gaze. Not one.

If I had quit then, I would never have forgiven myself. I would have regretted it my entire life. I would never be able to look someone in the eye and say I rode the Tour de France.

> I would have been the guy who rode *most* of the Tour de France and didn't complete it and I certainly wouldn't be telling you this story now.

At 10.50 p.m. I staggered into the hotel to tumultuous applause from the rest of the faster riders. They were showered, massaged and fed but they knew exactly what I had achieved. I had simply done it a bit more slowly. And that is what it feels like to conquer your fears, to ignore your excuses and remain committed to your goal when you want to quit. Please remember this as you go through this next chapter.

Giving up alcohol is not actually something you have to *work* at, in the way that you would train to run a marathon. You simply have to stop doing something, so it should be easy, shouldn't it? Well if it were 'easy', you would have done this already! And also, millions of others whose lives are blighted by alcohol would be able to simply move on. But we don't. In fact, there is a single reason behind why this isn't as easy as simply stopping. FEAR.

Change can be scary. Giving things up that we have told ourselves we need, sometimes for decades can be frankly terrifying! There are many books on the subject of fear and my personal favourite is *Feel The Fear And Do It Anyway* by Susan Jeffers – a life-changing and empowering book that shows up fear for what it really is – False Expectation Appearing Real.

In the vast majority of instances, our fears don't come anywhere *close* to being realised. They exist in our imagination, keeping us stuck and stopping us moving on, no matter how bad things are. Why? Because we think the alternative will be *worse*. So, a big part of this journey is to move forward through the process of change, managing our fears appropriately, accepting this will be unfamiliar territory, but that a better life is waiting on the other side of them.

You have heard me talk about the descent into alcohol addiction. Imagine you have descended into a pit and the only way out is up a huge staircase, hidden inside a tower. The top of this tower is shrouded in clouds as it seems so far away and it is so imposing that we feel like we cannot climb it. It is too tall, and the top of the tower is obscured, so we don't know if it is even worth the effort.

So, we remain stuck, rooted to the spot, looking up at this huge edifice, and the excuses come:
'I doubt it will even be worth it.'
'I don't know what to expect.'
'I don't like heights.'
'I don't like stairs.'
'I don't like lifts.'
'I bet you can't see anything from up there anyway.'
'At least I know what to expect down here.'
'All my drinking buddies are here so I won't be alone – there mightn't be anyone else up there, and if there are, I may not like them.'

Of course, this is a metaphor, but you can see how this works.

What we need is a simple process that can guide us through this uncertain journey, allow us to face the things that we need to face, and speed us on our way through the less critical parts.

THE TOWER OF TERROR

OK, so let's get on to that Tower of Terror that I've been talking so much about.

To the untrained eye, this tower seems so tall, its top is so shrouded in the clouds, that it seems almost like an unattainable goal. When I talk about 'terror', I'm not talking about hiding behind the sofa, like the first time you saw the Cybermen as a kid with Doctor Who, or whichever scary kids' TV show you used to watch. This is very different to how you would feel watching *The Shining* or *Saw* or one of these profoundly scary movies.

This kind of terror is the most insidious, subtle, fear – the kind that plays on your own *specific* fears. It is those fears that stop you actually making a change and taking action. It is the kind of fear that stops you getting the change that you want in your life.

It seems at first glance that this tower is just about un-climbable.

In actual fact, there are fourteen floors. The fourteenth floor is up above the clouds and that is where you will achieve your salvation. It is where you will have conquered your fears. But there are thirteen floors between you and it and they all need to be traversed. Some of them will be quite challenging for you.

Some of them may not feel particularly bothersome at all.

This journey will be very different for each of us. What scares me may not scare you, and vice versa. In order to get to that fourteenth floor, you have to pass the thirteen preceding ones via the stairs. I'm going to lead you through them one by one so that you're aware of them, and so that you can make plans for them. You can conquer them all by breaking them down individually and tackling them one at a time. A bit like climbing the Alpe D'Huez! So, don't worry. This is the basis of all human fears and you can identify which ones are relevant for you on this journey.

The first floor – The Physical Floor

This is where you might have a physical reaction to the fact that you're no longer drinking alcohol. In many ways this is the most straightforward of all the floors because it takes care of itself over time. All you have to do is not drink alcohol.

The human body is an amazing thing. It will heal, but it can have a stress response to removing the alcohol it has become so used to over the years, or even decades. This is something you've been experiencing through a craving, which you have tended to satisfy with an alcoholic beverage. Only now, you're actually taking that a step further and you're pushing your body a little bit further. This craving will get worse before it gets better.

While this is not great news, your body is *more than capable* of getting through this. If you are in any way worried, go and see your doctor. The sort of symptoms that you may experience are things like anxiety, shaking, headache, insomnia, fever and sweating. Your heart can race or feel quite irregular, and you may get elevated blood pressure as well. Any of these can be stressful in their own way, but they are very transient and the vast majority of people will just come through them. As your body recovers, everything will correct itself.

If you feel you need some medical supervision, then by all means seek it out. Some of the symptoms can be very severe and include seizures for those who have been drinking extremely large amounts on a non-stop basis.

For most people, a relaxing environment with the support of good friends and family will help them through it. Keep drinking healthy fluids and eating good nutritious food. Treat yourself like a tender young child in these early days and do everything you can to protect yourself from the worst of it and to stay safe. Thankfully, at the time of writing, I have not seen one person suffer a severe reaction to stopping drinking, but I also know that statistically – speaking, I am fortunate in this. Doing this will help your body in that repairing and healing process.

Remember that this body has taken all the poison you could throw at it, so we know it is made of strong stuff, but abstinence will be strange for it until it gets used to the new, better reality. After a period of between four and seven days, your body will be virtually clear of the poison that you put into it. Some of the effects will take a little bit longer. Your liver starts to recover and detoxification happens.

There will be an acute phase that may want to make you fall at the first hurdle – these are the kind of things that you can expect. I will remind you of this and it is really important:

> ## THIS IS *NOT* WHAT SOBRIETY FEELS LIKE!
> # ALCOHOL DID THIS TO YOU.
> ## VOW TO *NEVER* HAVE TO GO THROUGH THIS AGAIN.

If you have a rough time, make a note in a diary of exactly how you are feeling. In the days and weeks to come, when you begin to doubt yourself – read it. Consider this a love letter to yourself reminding you of what you are letting go.

Now we move onwards to floors two to thirteen. These are the *really* important ones. I am not saying that the physical side of things is not important. Far from it.

The majority of us have had an alcohol-free week or an alcohol-free month at some point and we've survived the process.

It seems quite clear that we can handle it, as we may have been here before. Perhaps we should rename this floor, 'Bloody awful, but not really scary'.

It is the psychological and emotional aspects that are the ones that most people find it most difficult. This next floor is the first of what I call, 'The Dirty Dozen' – the common human fears that hold us back from our dreams, goals and aspirations.

Welcome to Floor Two – The Fear of Rejection

This rejection can take many forms such as rejection by your friends, your so-called drinking buddies, or even members of your family. It could be that there is a regular post-work drinking frenzy where you are employed.

I have had a whole host of experiences with regard to different people's reactions to my not drinking anymore. I will touch on this again in the final part of the book, as we talk through maintaining momentum. This can be a very real issue and it can take some adjustment.

When you break each of these scenarios down, they are quite easy to deal with, but all together they can feel insurmountable. Don't worry – we will take time to walk through them one at a time.

Let's take a hypothetical example of *change* to examine what is going on.

I'm not trying to be gender specific or sexist about this but please play along with the metaphor and reverse the gender roles if you need to: Take the example of a happily married woman who has put on quite a lot of weight in the course of having children and looking after the family. She is not very happy with her body, and she has decided to make a change with regard to that. She may do a fantastic job of getting herself down to the gym, adjusting her diet and losing a lot of the weight. She looks better and feels better about herself. You may well say, *'Well that sounds great! Well done her, and I bet her husband/partner is delighted!'*

What we can see in many different situations is that that kind of change can be quite unsettling for people. This in turn can lead to a subtle shift in the relationship and a bit of discomfort. Perhaps the partner now feels inferior if she is attracting compliments from other people, including men. Perhaps the partner may question her motives around the sudden change and wonder if this is leading to something cataclysmic in terms of their relationship. Perhaps the partner may start to feel rejected, judged and inadequate himself.

Without good communication, you could see how mountains could be built from the smallest of molehills. Change can be threatening if not handled sensitively.

I would love to tell you that everyone will be happy for you but they won't.

Some people will watch you closely, secretly willing you to fail. They want you to start drinking again or to become a non-drinking, judgmental overly pious zealot. They will feel that if you succeed, this could make you better than them in their eyes. Their ego does not like that one bit.

Unfortunately, you cannot depend on *anyone but yourself* to react helpfully to this brave and amazing journey you have started out on. Of all the floors in this tower, this is possibly the one that affects the greatest proportion of people and, as such, it becomes the main reason why we feel pressure to crumble and capitulate.

Will I still be invited on nights out?
Will I still be invited on the boys' annual fishing trip?

Do I have to drop out of the forthcoming stag/hen weekend, as nobody will want me around?

So, how do we overcome this?

A bit of proactivity is needed. Turning up at the pub on a Friday night when your friends are all drinking heavily is going to be a tough gig in the early stages. Perhaps sitting a couple of evenings out while you find your feet and build your confidence is a good idea.

I should say at this point, that if these friends are purely 'drinking buddies' think carefully about how much you actually want to pursue them. If this is all that holds the group together then you have already outgrown them. Groups form so we can feel better about our addiction. Misery does indeed love company and, if you are out of control with your drinking, where is the one place you feel vindicated and welcome? Of course – with other out-of-control drinkers.

It is said we become the sum total of the seven people we spend the most time with. If your friendship group is made up solely of the heavy-drinking, 'must get out of the house' brigade, then guess what you will become? If your female friends are the 'wine o'clock mums' who go crazy on a Friday night and spend the rest of the weekend irritably nursing a hangover before doing it all again, guess where you will end up?

So, what does proactivity look like? Well, you need to plan ahead. Going on a lads golfing trip to Spain? Invited on a girls' boozy weekend at a spa? Work out who your allies are. Is there someone who will really understand and support you, at least while they are sober and thinking straight? Get them while they are sober and ask for them to support you. If they won't, maybe they weren't really your friend. What is your 'story' going to be? You need to have something you feel comfortable about sharing and that you can stick to. Some people make up stories about being on antibiotics and while that is initially plausible it becomes a little difficult to justify two months down the line! So be careful when lying to avoid the painful questions.

At some point, you will get a lot of pressure from a drunk so-called friend and you are going to need to be robust in resisting them. Doing that while lying takes a lot of nerve and will make you feel bad about the deception, so a half-truth is better than a no-truth, and it still gives you something to hang your integrity on.

Ironically, the reactions that I have had from my friends that have been most painful have generally been because that friend has been drunk at the time.

My personal favourites when in my local pub in Shetland were, 'Whit da *fuck* is wrang wi' dee?!' (or 'What appears to be the problem?' in sober English).

This was closely followed by, *'Can you nae HANDLE it?!'* from a man so completely out of it, his eyes were bloodshot and crossed and he was clinging on to the bar so tightly, to avoid keeling over, that I thought he would leave finger marks in the mahogany.

Of course, I couldn't handle it, and neither could he. His notion of 'handling it' is a total fabrication that I no longer have to lie to myself about.

That whole scene was dripping in irony and far from making me question what I was doing, it served to reinforce my decision. But when you catch your friends on a sober day they tend to be much more inquisitive. They're much more curious about what you're doing and why you're doing it that they actually tend to be more supportive and dare I say, a little bit envious.

'Oh, I don't think I could do that,' (They probably couldn't – yet).

'Are you now going to be pulling us up on the rubbish we talk?' (They accept the reality and yet still cling to their drinking).

A lot of that envy will come out as a reaction when people are drunk because they don't like feeling that emotion, and the alcohol has removed their ability to hold on to the feeling without expressing it – often through the form of passive aggression or inappropriately hurtful comments.

People really don't like the thought that they might be put under some form of scrutiny, which they are not comfortable applying to themselves. We are all on our own journey and it's not about lording your new reality over people, no matter how amazing you are feeling. Remember you were just as stuck as they are, and you probably wouldn't have responded very well to an 'ex-drinker' coming over as 'holier than thou'.

Even though you end up feeling sorry for the people who are still stuck in the cycle of addiction, be the shining example you wish once had been shown to you. Those who are ready will come to you.

Floor 3 – The Fear of Being Wrong

Well done! You've made it as far as the third floor and you are progressing.

Hiding for you on the third floor of the Tower of Terror is the fear of being wrong. I have already challenged you an awful lot around your assumptions as we've gone through this book and I am not going to stop now.

This is a process of rewiring that amazing, wonderful biocomputer that lies between your ears. Decades of acceptance of untruths are being laid bare and by now I hope you are finding a degree of comfort with that process. By letting go of our ego, new information is taken on its merits and considered carefully, rather than being dismissed out of hand just because it is new. All of those assumptions that you've held so dear while you've been drinking alcohol, on which you've had dependence, are being dismantled. The emperor is truly naked. And that can feel a little stressful in itself.

I used to say that for me alcohol felt like an old friend, a warm blanket to wrap myself against the cold, hard realities of the world and life. To wake up to the fact that that is not the case, while this is very empowering, you do question yourself a little bit in terms of how could you been so gullible or even stupid (not a particularly helpful word, but you are probably feeling it). I know I certainly felt a degree of anger at myself with regard to all those things about which I was making totally incorrect assumptions.

In fact, the anger I felt towards myself put me at risk of derailing this whole process, which makes this such an important floor for many people. The fear of being wrong and opening yourself up to that kind of self-scrutiny, which we will deal with in upcoming floors, is a very real one. It will hold you back if you don't acknowledge and deal with it.

Some of the things that you considered to be true and which you now know aren't true can require some mental adjustment as well. As you progress through your coming days and weeks of sobriety (another reason why a break is essential, whatever your long-term goals) you will be gathering evidence which now supports your new understanding. You will finally see the 'Emperor's New Clothes' for what they really are.

> 'In the kingdom of the blind, the one – eyed man is king.'
> Desiderius Erasmus

When you get to the end of this book, if you have signed up for the online bonuses, you can see how to continue this journey from a position of curiosity around other enabling truths that you can discover to keep you moving forward in life.

Floor Four – The Fear of the Unknown

There are a number of reasons as to why I chose a tower to represent the fears we face, one of which is that its summit can be so high, as to be obscured by clouds.

We don't know if the roof garden is *above* the clouds or *in* the clouds, i.e.: will the view be spectacular, or rubbish – at this stage we simply don't know. We don't even know how tall the tower actually is! But we do know that it *has* a roof garden, and we know that it does *have* a summit. As you climb the steps to the Fourth Floor, if you look out the window, you can already see down to the street below and see just how far you've come.

When you look up, it looks like there's quite a long way to go. Don't worry because we've got it all covered. You haven't come this far only to go this far and no further. If you've been drinking heavily for a long period of time like I did, you don't really know what you're going to feel like without that crutch.

How will you cope without that false friend?
What does your life actually look like without that unhealthy routine?
How will you cope without that 'little reward' that you gave yourself?
This can feel scary.

This is probably one of the most consistently disabling fears that people have.

The interesting thing about this floor is that it exists only in your imagination. By definition, anything that is in the future is unknown, by virtue of the fact it hasn't happened yet! When

112

people who have been through the online programme discuss 'their tower', this one tends to figure quite highly. I often become quite mischievous with people over this, as it is actually the best way to deal with it. I pose lots of questions and I would encourage you to have a go with some of these too.

Them: 'What will my friends say? I think they will reject me.'

Me: 'I'm sorry I don't know your friends so I can't answer that. Neither do you, so you can't answer that either, unless you are telepathic. Are you telepathic? What am I thinking as I write this?'

Of course, I am empathetic in the overall context, but actually a gentle 'shake' is what we need on this as we simply attach ourselves to our worst fears, which virtually *never* come to pass.

Another fear could be:

Them: 'How will I get through the Christmas party/wedding/family meal etc. – I don't know how I will cope without alcohol.'

Me: 'It's a fair point – they could all turn on you, see right through what you are trying to do, tie you down and pour gin down your throat using a funnel. Or maybe a few of them will simply make a couple of silly comments then get pissed and not even notice? You may get an early night, go to bed hydrated and wake up feeling awesome. If that is your worst-case scenario, I would take that!'

By using humour, we look at our perceptions in a slightly different way and our fears instantly lose their power over us. If you can adopt a position of curiosity, this can become an educational, and even exciting part of your journey.

Only you really know why you made this decision. You know how bad it was and what literally forced you to make a change. Things got so bad for *you* that *you* felt *you* had to act. You took a wonderfully inspired, brave and empowering decision to change an aspect of your life. That is a *wonderful* position to be in, because everything is back in play in your life.

All of those things that were not possible, because you had a dependence on alcohol are now back on the table. By making this one change, your life is on a different path. A better path. Maybe you are not going to run a marathon, climb Mount Everest, or do silly things like riding the Tour de France.

Or maybe you are.

That is the beauty of the unknown. The unknown is where the infinite abundance of possibilities lie. Worrying about the as yet unknown reaction of Uncle Joe, who has never done anything of significance in his life, is you being unfair to your own greatness. With regard to the Tour de France, for me it was one of the things that really symbolised that 'this is my new reality'.

I could never have done that without making a significant change with regard to alcohol and now I've done it. More people climb Mount Everest every year than ride the course of the Tour. I'm not saying that you need to find such an emblematic thing to do to prove to yourself who you are, but I would insist that you explore the possibilities. What have you dreamt of doing but talked yourself out of?

Why not use this chapter as a diagnostic tool for your goals after you have finished your run-through of this book. These fears are universal. This is not just about alcohol because combinations of these floors stop us doing everything in life.

Curiosity is *kryptonite* for the fear of the unknown.

Floor 5 – Fear of the Limelight

Nobody particularly likes being put in the spotlight unless it is on their own terms. I sometimes quite enjoy it in a work environment. I have always been the one that has been happy to get up on stage and do the big presentations in front of hundreds of people – I actually get quite a buzz from it.

I also know that the fear of public speaking is one of the most common fears that many people have and they tend to shy away from the limelight. Using my own personal example, I'm really happy, in a work environment where I'm confident of my subject, to go and stand up and communicate that to a huge audience. But there are other areas in my life which I *really* don't like a light being shone into. There are some things that I'm not so proud of, and that can be a very real fear for people.

When people start to understand what you're doing and that you've made this change to abstinence, you do start to enter the spotlight and attract attention. Some of the reactions will be very positive and some may be quite negative. A lot of people, when they're not drunk, will be quite envious and will be curious about what you're doing. So, you have to get ready for those questions. You can't change this; you can just get ready for it. Everyone who has been through this journey has come up against this at some point.

Never forget, this is your choice to do this for yourself, not for them. You don't owe anybody an explanation, no matter how much they may seek it.

Sometimes if people are being persistently belligerent about this, I play a little game with them. I say, *'No thanks I don't smoke'*.

When the confusion takes hold, and they seek clarification, I say *'Oh sorry I misheard you – I don't drink either.'*

These days, nobody would force a cigarette upon you, although they would have done forty years ago. Very subtly, you have just reminded them that drinking alcohol and smoking tobacco are essentially the same thing – a short-term addictive 'pleasure hit' that society sees as acceptable in certain situations.

Forty years ago, you would have been pressured into drinking even if you were driving. Times change.

Your own acceptance of your new reality will start to solidify as you find you have to justify it and, yes, you will have to answer the same question over and over and over again, I'm sure. But as you go through that it starts to become easier, and you'll start to really *live* your new reality. Take *every* opportunity that you can to enjoy it because you are doing a wonderful thing. Over the coming weeks and months, the narrative will begin to shift. Many people will come up to you and say, *'You know what, I'm actually quite inspired by what you're doing,'* and that is rewarding, so take the time to fully appreciate what you are doing.

These people mean it when they say it. They know they are addicted, but cannot as yet make the step you have done. They do not yet possess your strength.

> # YOU'D BE SURPRISED WHO'S WATCHING YOUR JOURNEY & BEING INSPIRED BY IT. DON'T QUIT.

Floor Six – The Fear of Loss

This is a very powerful fear that will inhibit people from making a change. Note, this is the *fear* of loss, not an actual loss, which is an important difference. The things that you think you are losing are probably quite obvious to you at this moment in time and yet what you're *gaining* is yet to come and thus less clear.

This feels like a real disparity. If you have ever changed jobs, the first day on your new job, or while you're working a notice period from your old job, can feel really weird and scary. If you've ever been in that situation, when you have handed your notice in on the old job and you get that euphoric feeling of excitement and you will be thinking, '*YES, I've committed. I'm on my way!*'

And then the doubts creep in. You know what you are losing, but you do not yet know what the new job is really going to be like. *What if they were lying in the interview to get you to sign? What if the new boss is an even bigger bully than the old one?*

All of a sudden, no matter how miserable you were in the old job, you get a sudden urge to jump back, however fleeting. *'Better the devil you know,'* encapsulates this quite nicely.

It is exactly the same with alcohol, this perceived 'old friend' or 'comfort blanket'. All of a sudden feel like you will miss these, and the rose-tinted spectacles go on. If you are regularly going out for drinks after work with colleagues, you know that this is going to feel different if you are not consuming alcohol yourself. It will take some adjustment and we get fearful of that.

What is there to be scared of, really? A couple of questions on the first couple of occasions, but that is it. But, at this point, you've got a sense that you're giving something up without actually fully understanding what the future looks like. So, you need to tough this one out a little bit.

That's probably not necessarily what you want to hear, but this is a time when you need some stamina. You did the Life Balance Disc and you know full well what you are in for. Don't fall at the first hurdle just because you have no certainty over the future. Even if you stayed exactly where you are, you still have no certainty over the future, so why not do things on your own terms?

By way of example, consider the story of Martine Wright:

On 7th July 2005, Martine Wright left her London home, as usual, nursing a slight hangover. She was heading to work on the Tube, having boarded at Moorgate Underground station. Wearing brand new white trainers, she grabbed a copy of the free newspaper, found a seat and settled into her journey, paying little heed to her fellow passengers.

At 8.49 a.m. one of those passengers detonated a suicide bomb, one of several devices used in a co-ordinated attack that would claim fifty-two lives that morning.

Martine recalls looking up at the ceiling, puzzled at why one of her new trainers was covered in red and embedded in the twisted metal of the ceiling. She would later discover that it still contained her foot. Another passenger's foot was embedded in her thigh.

When she is interviewed, she often talks about the impact that moment, and the massive injuries, had on her life. While she hesitates to say it is the 'best' thing that happened to her, she certainly believes that it was a significant turning point in her life that opened up a huge number of possibilities for her.

Now she is a Paralympian, has met the Queen and Prince Philip at a garden party at Buckingham Palace and has a wonderful husband and son.

'People ask me if I would turn the clock back. Part of me says: 'Yeah, it would be nice to have my legs back'. But my life now is so amazing. I've had the opportunity to do so much, meet so many people. I don't think I would turn that clock back if I had the chance.'

My point? She herself says that if that bomb had not detonated, she would have carried on in her humdrum life, and we would not know her name. The injury didn't define her, it allowed her to show who she truly was.

So, don't kid yourself that staying in the same place is any guarantee of things remaining the same. Some people do become a little bit unfamiliar around you and a bit nervous of the change you have initiated. There is a sense of, 'What am I going to do when I have a really stressful moment?' (or whatever your trigger was for reaching for the bottle). Uncomfortable truth time – alcohol makes you *lazy*.

We are creatures of habit. For years we have simply used one option – drinking – out of a *near-infinite* number of possible activities to cope in a given situation. Now is the time to reopen our eyes to the wonderful and better alternatives. As we move through the other floors, you will start to see that this floor fits in with the overall context of all the others.

That fourteenth floor as the goal, *massively* outweighs anything that you may be holding on to in the short term. But you will feel loss, and that is OK. Just be ready for it, be aware of it and let it go.

Floor Seven - The Fear of Being Judged

Congratulations, you are now halfway up the Tower of Terror. Take a look out of that window again and take your first glimpse of the top. It is appearing through the clouds and you can actually see the goal. Dealing with these fears has been nothing more than a process and by breaking them down into individual chunks, we have made the whole thing manageable. If you look down, then you see that the distance down to the ground below is exactly the same as what is to come. There are still floors to deal with, but we are making progress.

The next thing we will deal with is the fear of being judged. People will make their own mind up about what you are doing, based on their own experiences and beliefs. Some people might say, *'What's the problem here – are you an alcoholic?'*
'Were you just not able to cope?'
'Has your boss told you that you are drinking too much and you stink of alcohol in the morning?'
'Has your partner delivered you an ultimatum?'

Everybody will be thinking all these different things because they are trying to make sense of the situation. Only you know the reality of the situation, and they don't. The judgments that people make about you say everything about *them*, and absolutely nothing about *you*. It is human nature to seek to make sense of everything. Let me give you an example:

Let's say you look up into the sky, and you see some clouds up there.
Your brain is *always* trying to make a shape out of them. Does that look like a car? a horse's head? or something even more

abstract? We are always trying to make sense of the world – we're always trying to put things into a 'box' and prove to ourselves that we understand it. Only you know why you are making the change. Everyone else is merely speculating and guessing.

You may choose to share your 'why' with people who judge you if it's important to you to put them straight, and that is, of course your choice. I would counsel against doing that too much, particularly in the early stages.

Your new-found sobriety is like lighting a fire in the wilderness. You start with a spark, an inspiration, and through diligent effort and focus, turn it into an ember and then a small flame. You coax and nurture it, putting bigger and bigger twigs and branches on until it's a roaring blaze. If you throw all the big logs on straight away the fire will go out.

When I was growing up, there was a phrase that was used to describe people who took great pleasure in undermining your goals. They were called 'Bonfire pissers' because they liked pissing on your bonfire because they didn't have one of their own. The best way that you prove the judges wrong is by simply being the person that you want to be.

In my experience, when people say to me. *'Wow Andy, you look different. Your eyes are clearer, and your skin less blotchy,'* or *'You've lost weight', it serves to hugely reinforce the fact that I have made the right decision. These tend to be unprompted compliments born out of curiosity, and maybe even a little envy.*

I'm not a perfect specimen of humankind by any stretch of the imagination, but I do look different to how I used to look and people notice that, and say I look younger. I am sure you will agree that that is a better kind of judgment, and believe me when I say that it does come in time.

That is when the interesting conversation starts. They will ask, *'What's your secret?'* When you tell them that you have given up drinking alcohol that can really throw them. This is a very different discussion now because there is irrefutable evidence that quitting drinking makes you look and feel better and, provided you haven't become a judgmental asshole in the process, this will really make them think. Nobody can argue with it – it's how you feel, and is absolutely impossible to be challenged. So whatever people's judgment, simply say, *'You know what, I did this, and I feel better'*.

Thank them for their kind comments and for saying you look better, and say: *'Inside I just feel loads better. And it's the best thing I ever did.'*

Unless they have a real problem, that's all you need to say to anybody who judges you – even if you don't feel you are quite there yet. My experience in the months and years since I stopped is that the benefits keep stacking up. Sometimes it creeps up on you and you are not even aware of it. Over time, this just gets better and better and better. People adjust and accept the new you, and life moves on.

In the early days you might have to 'front it out' a little bit and just say, *'Yeah I feel really great'*. The alternative is perceived as a chink in your armour and they will pounce to put you back in the little box, which their ego tells them that you should be in.

There are other charity sobriety programmes where you can start to make this more about the charity than yourself. This can certainly help in the early days, and then you can say, *'I felt good so I am continuing.'* When it comes to actually making a lasting change to your drinking these high-profile 'SoberOctober'-type campaigns tend to be ineffective, but there is never any downside to a month off the poison, so many people use it as an excuse for a break.

But it feels like you're doing something quite noble when you flash the charity wristband and it's good to get that reinforcement. Or you can do something crazy like sign up for the Tour de France and nobody questions your drinking then!

In short, if signing up for an activity helps you manage other people then go for it. In time, you will realise what **you** think and feel is the only thing that matters.

Floor Eight – The Fear of Commitment

Welcome to floor eight – you are well over halfway. Now, when you look up and see the top of the tower, just visible through the clouds, it's actually closer than the ground down below. You can feel that growing sense of anticipation of what it's going to be like in your new life.

You are going to have more energy. You are going to have more money. Your health will improve in ways you didn't even expect and so much more. This is an awesome and brave thing that you're doing, and it's now completely within your grasp.

On this floor, we need to accept that we all fear commitment from time to time. We all fear being locked or tied down. We say to ourselves that nothing will ever be the same again. But let's think about that for a moment – what exactly are you committing to? I have said to people on many occasions that I now feel *completely* in control of my feelings towards alcohol.

Do I drink alcohol routinely? No.
Do I miss it? No.
Do I think about it? Virtually never. And I used to think about it *all* the time.
Have I ever had a drink since I stopped? Yes, and generally for the reason that I'm toasting somebody's health, and I simply do not wish to impose my decision on others if there are no soft drinks around. If people are passing round the champagne, I have a centimetre in the bottom of the glass, and I will take a sip, because I will honour what they have achieved. That is just my personal view, as I don't want to muddy those waters with regard to having to explain myself. Things are just *easier*. Note the

centimetre. At no point will I fool myself into thinking, 'just the one'. In terms of 'take it or leave it', I do both. Does this mean I have 'fallen off the wagon'? Of course not. I did it on my own terms with full awareness. That is what FREEDOM means to me.

I once got into a debate with an AA member who was adamant that this sip put me back at 'Day One' again, and that this was failure. To me, it felt the opposite. This was success, my new empowered self taking control of what was going on.

Does this sip lead to a craving? Absolutely not but this has been a long journey and I am now in a *very* different place from where I started. I don't particularly enjoy the sip, but I'm doing it for a reason and it's not about me, it's about somebody else. I don't feel bad about it, it doesn't change how I feel about alcohol not one little bit, but it's just a choice.

You may choose your circumstances in which you feel it's acceptable to have a drink, but by now you should fully understand alcohol for what it is.

As a recreational and readily available toxic substance, it is extremely disadvantageous to consume it. There may be some times when you think you are willing to forgo that under certain circumstances. This is of course the worst thing you can possibly do in the first few months, as the old programmes in your subconscious mind are still running. 'Just the one', when it is for the wrong reasons, is the epitaph for many an ex-drinker's downfall.

So why even mention this at all? Because the fear of commitment to a life with zero alcohol in it for evermore may feel like too big an undertaking at this early stage. Organisations like Alcoholics Anonymous have 'A Day At A Time' as the cornerstone of their approach and while I do not agree with it *at all* in the longer term, it is exactly how this battle must be fought in the early stages. If AA had an exit strategy, I may have found it more viable for me. As it was, I found the 'never again' notion too much to comprehend at the outset – I had to arrive at that conclusion

myself. So, a key element is to keep an open mind. Convinced you don't want to totally give up? No problem – just give yourself a break of three months and then see how you feel – you have your entire life in front of you. An open mind and a sense of curiosity has led thousands of people to make an empowered decision.

Being able to 'take it or leave it' means you have found the ability to *leave* it.

It's just different. You're not committing to anything. This is your new normality.

Once you make that decision and change your viewpoint, you reprogramme your subconscious mind.

Your subconscious and the feelings within it, have prevented change for so many years. Now, by understanding what you are trying to achieve, it actually prevents you from going back to the old reality. You look on a glass of alcohol the way, a non-smoker looks at a cigarette, or a non-junkie would view a syringe full of heroin. It's just something that other people do. This approach takes no effort and it takes no continued commitment. It's just the way it is now for you. Drinking heavily is hard work. From a personal standpoint, I was probably putting more effort into being a drinker than I ever had to after I stopped. Not having to worry about it is much easier!

Typical worries were:

Where am I getting that evening's alcohol from?

Have I got enough money in my wallet to go and get a bottle of wine?

Am I going to be able to get to the off licence on the way home if I am working late?

All that stuff takes *effort* and it is exhausting and annoying. So, in taking a break from the booze, what are you actually *committing* to? In the early days you are committing to a bit of self-discipline and committing to being kind to yourself.

After that you are committing to happiness and to life. I have a feeling you won't find anything to be scared of in that.

Floor Nine - The Fear of Money

We are absolutely flying up the Tower of Terror and we're not even out of breath! We've dealt with all the previous floors and tackled them head on. By remaining calm and resourceful we see that those fears were at best imagined, and at worst able to be tackled by breaking them down into bitesize chunks.

We're all different and on our own journey. We all have our own pressure points and our own motivations for doing *anything* in our lives. This is part of being human, and it is really cool. Floor nine is all about the fear of money.

This may seem like a strange one to have here, but these floors represent universal fears that stop us doing anything, so it is important to consider *everything*.

This fear of money is closely related to the fear of success, which we will cover later. Fear of money can stem from when you are told as a child that money is the root of all evil, or perhaps that rich people are greedy. The pursuit of money is fairly unwholesome but the fact remains that if you're spending several hundred pounds a month on alcohol, which can equate to thousands of pounds a year, you're going to have more of it when you quit.

You might want to take this moment to consider that. Is that a good thing, a bad thing, or don't you care? You may want to consider what you would do with more money. It might be for a family holiday, a particular possession, a new car, a motorbike, to give some money to charity or you're saving for your child's education. Acquisition of money for its own sake is rarely seen as helpful, so how would you turn it into a positive?

Think back to your Life Balance Disc – did anything jump out that needs investing in? Maybe it's just paying off the credit card debts. If it is that, every time you are feeling low, remember that rather than literally pouring your money down the toilet, you are in fact buying peace of mind. All because of this wonderful decision you have taken.

A little while ago I saw a picture of myself from over twenty years ago and I looked at the youthful face staring back at me. It prompted an interesting question – what would I have had that guy do differently? I concluded that most things worked out in the end, however painful they were at the time, so probably not much. Apart from the drinking. Boy, what could I do with that completely wasted £100,000 now? All I bought with that was ill health and misery.

If I had given the money to that younger man, he would have probably gone off the rails with it. I certainly learned a lot about myself in the last couple of decades. Money will come into your life as a result of this change and it has its own energy, so put that to good use.

Floor Ten – The Fear of Conflict

This can be a very real thing. I personally have experienced a bit of it since I chose to stop drinking – generally from friends when they are drunk. Change can create conflict and this can feel threatening to you and other people. Any kind of change for better, particularly when it makes people consider deficiencies in themselves, can lead to a negative reaction. This can be very disabling, as nobody likes conflict – especially when we are tackling a difficult change ourselves.

I do, unfortunately, have stories highlighting this conflict from ex-drinker friends and colleagues who've come to the same conclusion about alcohol that I did. One of my very good friends used to go on regular weekend fishing trips with all his buddies. They would all go fishing and drink heavily. When he changed his habits, he stopped being invited and he struggled with the injustice of that. This is really sad and my heart went out to him.

On this journey you will genuinely find out who your friends really are. There will be friends who are supportive and there will be so-called friends who shun you because you no longer fit into that little box they wanted you to fit in to. Some proactivity can make a huge difference to minimise these kinds of experiences.

There is, however, a middle ground and my experience has led me to believe that these will be the majority of people you deal with. The truth is, this group simply *don't know what to say*. On one hand, they may be pleased for you but on the other, worried what this means for your relationship. They may also be worried that you are vulnerable, so are not sure if they can drink in your presence among their other concerns.

By way of a partially – related example, I have a very close friend who suffered sudden, total and catastrophic hearing loss. She literally woke up one morning and her hearing had disappeared. What an utterly terrifying place to be – a world of complete silence, and the sense of being struck down in your prime of life. Nobody knew what to say. What do you say to someone to whom something like that has happened?

I was chatting with her husband about it and he mentioned she was not in a good way and felt very isolated. So, I reached out to her via SMS and said I was thinking about her and that if there was anything I could do to help to please ask.

She responded, saying she was feeling alone. She had drafted a message she was planning on sending via social media to let everyone know what had happened but was unsure whether to send it. I encouraged her to do so as I hadn't really known what to say and even sending my initial message had felt a little risky.

She did send it and the response was an avalanche of empathy, support, love and admiration for her beautifully written account of how she was doing. It broke the ice, and the sense of relief among her friends was palpable.

If I hadn't spoken to her husband, I wouldn't have sent the initial message and she may not have posted her story.

By posting her situation on social media, she gave everyone an opportunity to engage – from simply 'liking' her message to a huge love-filled reply of support. Everyone felt able to express their feelings towards her, and she no longer felt alone, or that she needed to explain herself over and over.

You can learn from her. Be **proactive** about this. Reassure people that you won't be judging them, and tell them that this is your decision, not theirs.

Let them know that this changes nothing about your friendship with them in your eyes and that you hope that they will feel the same. Tell them if they have any questions, then please ask, otherwise simply tell them you hope you can count on their support. You cannot rely on them to do this for you and by being proactive, you also control your story and get to set the tone. Be ready for the fact that some people may feel a little threatened by it. The way that you overcome that is by simply being kind to them and to yourself.

I often have to say to people I am in no way judgmental about people who are drinking and I really mean that. I would be the biggest hypocrite in the world if I turned into a pious, judgmental asshole that had 'seen the light' and sought to criticise others. Then my friends would judge me in return, and desert me in droves, with good reason.

As we go through this, I know I'm pretty full on with regard to letting you know the downsides of drinking too much. At the same time, I'm not ever going to say to somebody, 'You should not drink!' If someone had said that to me when I was drunk, there was probably a real danger I would have done or said something I regretted! For clarity, if I had my wish you would never drink alcohol again, but that is my ego (more on this later) talking. I simply want you to live your best life – whatever that looks like.

If you've not made that decision for yourself, it's pointless anyway. Even if you saw someone harming themselves, the best thing you can do is get strong, get healthy, look better and be a shining example. You will be surprised at the number of friends who then seek you out for help.

Be the person who looks better.
Be the person who looks younger.
Be the person who has more money.
Be the person who has more time.
Be the person who lives longer and has better health.
Be the person who is simply *calmer*.

"Our **deepest fear** is not that we are weak. Our deepest fear is that we are **powerful beyond measure.**
It is our **light**, not our darkness that most frightens us.
We ask ourselves, **who am I to be brilliant, gorgeous, talented, *fabulous*?**
Actually, who are you **not** to be?
You are a child of God.
Your playing small does not serve the world...
As we are liberated from our own fear, our presence automatically **liberates others**"

From Marianne Williamson's "A Return To Love"
As Quoted by Nelson Mandela in his inaugural speech, 1994

Floor Eleven – The Fear of Failure

It may be that this is not the first time you tried to make a change with regard to how much you've been drinking. In fact, the likelihood is that you have tried before and didn't manage it and now you are reading and being inspired (I hope) by this book.

There can be a huge sense of failure that goes along with this process. When you feel out of control about something and you try to take control back, if that control eludes you it can actually feel quite catastrophic. It really isn't a catastrophe at all. It is called *learning*.

I run a huge sober group on social media and people who are trying to quit by themselves or moderate their alcohol intake, often use words like, 'I failed again – Day 1 again for me.'

The sense of self-loathing is palpable. When people join the online programme, sometimes they say things like, 'This is my last roll of the dice,' as the sense of failing one more time will be the end.

I always appreciate the fact that people place a lot of faith in me and in this process. I know the process works as I have seen so many people use it to get their lives back. I hope that by now you know my own personal story. I am the living embodiment that, as somebody who failed many times, success is possible for you. Maybe you are facing down a real problem such as a key relationship's turning point or perhaps an ultimatum from your spouse or something like that and it feels like the stakes are really high. That's a scary place to be, but **this process works if you work the process.**

If you've come this far and you have kept an open mind, you will have understood that alcohol is an addictive substance. This results in both a physical and an emotional dependency. The physical side of things looks after itself once you are past the first few days, which is why we are focusing so much on the emotional side of things. This is where success in the longer term is to be found.

I hope by now you understand that your drinking problem is not your fault.

It's not because you're weak – you've just been caught in an ingenious trap. Success is there at your fingertips. It is within your grasp. You simply have to reach out and grab it, no matter what happens.

Is this a linear process, where everything gets better day by day? Not really. There will be steps forward and back. Does that mean a step back is failure? It does, if you let your EGO drive your feelings. Let me digress with a short story:

My youngest son, five years old at the time of writing, is currently learning to swim. Every Wednesday evening, we go to a small pool and he has swimming lessons.

Every week, I tell him the same thing:

'Listen to what the teachers say, and try your best to do what they tell you – you will get there.'

Young children are wonderfully devoid of ego. They have no sense of limitations, or expectations of what they can/can't do.

EVERYTHING is new to them and every day they learn at an extraordinary rate.

Learning is fun, and part of their daily routine.

There is also a lady in her sixties who has a lesson after him. She is a lovely woman and she is pushing herself to learn to swim – something that has evaded her for one reason or another her entire life.

That makes her completely awesome in my book and I have told her that very thing. Yet, every time we speak, she tells me how stupid she is, she recounts every tiny mistake that she made the prior week and that she feels a fool for having left it so long to learn. The difference? **Ego.**

In modern society, we tend to equate ego with a negative, narcissistic trait. The dictionary definition is *'A person's sense of self-esteem or self-importance.'* In psychoanalytic terms it is *'The part of the mind that mediates between the conscious and the unconscious and is responsible for reality testing and a sense of personal identity'.*

So, what does that mean? The lady has a sense that she *should* be able to do this, that my five-year-old son does not. While this is an admirable aspiration, it makes learning PAINFUL.

The more we can let go of the ego and simply accept what is, the easier this whole process becomes. We want the quick fix. We want to be a 'normal drinker', which actually doesn't exist. Those people we tend to hold up as role models of being able to have 'just the one' are actually people who rarely drink at all – it is simply not a significant part of their life.

Being able to 'Take it or leave it' means virtually *always* leaving it.

For those people that I work with on a personal basis, it's such a wonderful journey to be on – even with the inevitable ups and downs. We sometimes need to be told it's OK to stumble, providing that we use it to learn, rather than give up. Ironically, the fear of failure can sometimes make failure happen faster, because it stops us taking action and getting started.

On this journey, this is the *only* definition of failure. To never try, dooms us from the outset. Some organisations talk about 'falling off the wagon', and such like. I don't believe that there is any such thing as a wagon – just know that you're on *your* journey. You're on your way and you've made the decision. That is brave and amazing.

I have a reality check for you – you are NOT perfect and neither am I.

And that is OK.

Can I offer some advice based on the people I have seen go through this process to huge success? Some of the things you think are going to be incredibly difficult will be easy, and some of the things you think will be easy, will be tough.

This is the way of things. You simply do not know enough to predict how this is going to be. You will find strength you never knew you had in the dark moments, and you will find complacency creep in when you think you have got it sorted.

The fear of failing is generally far worse than the reality, so be kind to yourself.

You are so close to the end of this process because you've probably got ninety per cent of the tools that you need in order to make a lasting change which is going to be enormous in your life. There is still some mind-blowing stuff to come, but I hope you are feeling a renewed confidence that maybe, just maybe, a better life awaits you.

You've come too far to only come this far – keep going!

> *'Yesterday is history, tomorrow is a mystery, but today is a gift – this is why we call it the present.'*
> Master Oogway, Kung Fu Panda

Live in the present and don't get too attached to what is to come.

I am no fan of 'living a day at a time' as a long-term strategy, but in the early days, it is genuinely the only way.

Floor 12 – The Fear of Abandonment

Floor twelve is the fear of abandonment and this is a very core fear for many people. Human beings are very social animals. We need friends and family around us. Emotionally, we need to operate within a social circle because without this we start to wither and die.

In fact, many people who have come to the conclusion that they need to make a change with regard to alcohol are inherently lonely. The image of a heavy drinker being the life and soul of the party, surrounded by revelling friends, laughter and good times is very rarely true. Alcohol addiction is a lonely business, where the true extent of the suffering is often hidden from loved ones.

From my perspective, most of my heaviest drinking was reserved for when I was sitting alone, away from prying eyes and judgment. This can become a self-fulfilling prophecy. Most people do not wish to spend time with those who continually drink themselves into oblivion, and likewise, the heavy drinker loses all social confidence, preferring to simply mark time on their own with a bottle or a glass. Ironically, this also fuels a sense of abandonment. *What if my friends won't like me anymore if I am not drinking?*

Perhaps we have sought solace among other drinkers who do not judge or criticise for so long we have lost sight of what the alternative would look like?
Who will want to spend time with me, if I am sober? Will sober people want to spend time with me?

As our self-esteem crashes to ever deeper lows, we find ourselves paralysed by fear at the enormity of a sober social existence. In this new reality, you will certainly find out who your true friends are. Fellow addicts who sought strength in your mutual suffering may now feel challenged. Some may feel happy for you and say things like, 'I wish I could do that,' or they may express some scepticism, based on the fact they don't think they could do that. Some friends unfortunately think they know what is best for you. They cannot bear the thought that you could free yourself of this addiction. They may ridicule, or even try to actively sabotage you, especially while drunk themselves. These people are driven by their own egos; they are putting their own sense of self-importance over and above any feelings of support they may have for you as an individual. Where a friendship was based solely on alcohol consumption, and that was all there was in common, then you can expect big change to happen.

In these instances, you need new friends. Sorry but it is true. These people want you to fail, so they feel vindicated – just like the guys at the bottom of Le Alpe D'Huez who wanted me to join them in the van. If your 'saboteurs' are close family, this can feel like a very real problem and you will have to have a think about how you handle that one. Often an honest conversation while they are sober can be very cathartic. Saying something like, *'I need to do this because I am hating my drinking and want to make a change. I hope you will support me, as I don't think it's going to be easy. I don't need your support, but it would mean the world to me to have it,'* can work wonders and also smoke out any hidden questions or concerns they may have.

For what it is worth, the number one concern people tend to have is that they may be required to stop drinking too, or that it is going to be awkward having alcohol around you. By being proactive, you take the initiative. Very few heavy drinkers are comfortable with what they are doing and they will be intrigued, although unlikely to want to follow in your footsteps – yet.

Will you be ostracised at the next works' do? Will family shun you at the upcoming wedding?

In my experience, and those of the clients with whom I work, the reverse is true. The television presenter Adrian Chiles who made a BBC documentary about his drinking put it succinctly:

'I used to drink heavily and nobody ever mentioned it. Then I stopped drinking, and everyone wanted to talk about it.'

So, any fear of abandonment is quite ironic, as if anything it makes you the most fascinating person in the room!

I am much more engaging company without being 'blasted' and, whereas I used to feel that being the one sober person at a party was the loneliest place in the world, I realise now that that assumption was the work of cognitive dissonance again. By flipping my thinking around, I enjoyed answering questions, and very quickly perfected my 'story', which I could tailor to different individuals. I learned the way to close down a conversation when I didn't want to be bored senseless and I could also share my 'stupid shit I have done' drinking stories without any fear or embarrassment as I had moved on. It was simply like recounting a story of falling off my bike as a child.

I love the fact that these days I can have pleasant conversations with people from which I learn more about them and *remember* it. If they are drinking, it may get to a point where they become boring or overfamiliar and I would simply move on. I understand I used to be like that and it isn't pretty.

You will fear judgment and abandonment, so take steps to practise what you preach. Be kind, inclusive and attentive.

Shortly after I stopped drinking, we were at a weekend music festival with good friends and their families. There were many kids running around and the alcohol was flowing quite freely among the rest of the adults. I didn't miss the alcohol at all and, after we got home, one of my friends sent me a message to say how much more she had enjoyed the weekend, in the knowledge that if anything untoward were to happen, I was fully *compos mentis* and could sort the situation out if need be. I felt like Superman!

If loneliness has been an issue, take the extra time that you now have to start to explore your interests. Join the clubs you always wanted to, go to the gym, or start studying at a night class for that qualification you always talked yourself out of. By making empowered choices, the course of our life changes for the better.

Call the distant relative. Make the apology. Reach out to someone that you know is struggling. You will have time and energy on your side so put it to good use and begin to stretch your social muscles once more – gently at first – without a glass in your hand. Over time, the 'new you' in their eyes once more becomes 'you' only this time there is less guilt, less unpredictability, fewer rows and deeper relationships.

Over time the questions and the scepticism stop. I got quite a number of *'Are you still not drinking?'* questions but even the most determined sceptic gets tired of asking the same question to receive the same answer!

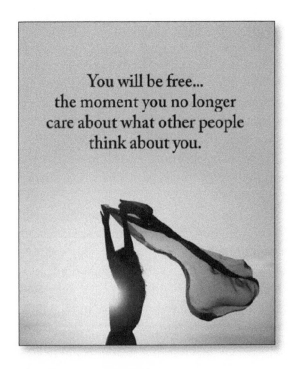

You will be free...
the moment you no longer
care about what other people
think about you.

Floor 13 – The Fear of Success

This is the final 'fear floor' which comes before you get on to the roof garden, out into the open air, where your salvation and your future lie. You begin to see this new world that you can barely remember seeing before. You see the world, perhaps as your inner child did, before the alcohol got its fingers into your soul.

This view of your future looks amazing!

But do you deserve amazing? Given that alcohol robs us of our self-confidence, the fear of success can be very real. It has taken a lot of courage to climb up the steps of the Tower of Terror. I applaud you beyond words.

There is a saying that those people who overcome addictions are the strongest people on the planet, and I personally believe that to be exactly the case. People have proven to me time and again that, with the right roadmap, they possess far more strength than they ever imagined. And you are one of those incredible people. So, what on earth is the fear of success?

Take the example of a lottery winner. There is an awful statistic that the majority of people who've had very little money and then win the lottery embark on a voyage of self-sabotage if they have no external help and support. The money has often gone within a two-year time frame purely and simply because they have not been equipped to deal with their new reality.

We all have a sense of what we deserve in these new circumstances and it can feel very strange indeed to be out of our comfort zone in this way. By considering this beforehand and equipping yourself, you take a more proactive approach in keeping with your beliefs and values. A study was recently conducted on this subject where a fake job advert was placed in a local newspaper. People applied and were invited for interview.

On the day of the interviews, the interviewer addressed all the candidates and said there had been a terrible mistake – a typo in the advert meant the stated salary was incorrect. Everybody groaned, eyes rolled and glances were exchanged. Everyone felt duped that they had been lured in under false promises. But then the interviewer did something unexpected. They said that the advert had missed a 'zero' off the figure and that the salary was, in fact, TEN times higher. The majority of people, even though they felt qualified right up until that point and able to do the job as stated, made their excuses and left. They simply walked out because their self-image would not allow them to believe they were worth a salary of that size. What would you have done in that situation? It is an interesting question, isn't it?

Instead of a £40,000 job that you may have felt was a reasonable promotion it was in fact a £400,000 a year chance of a lifetime. Would you embrace it or reject it? What negative self-talk might you have experienced to talk yourself out of it?

So, what if you finally become this new person? What does the sober and empowered you look like? What does that actually even mean? That can feel scary, so take this moment to start to consider how you will feel when you have conquered this. If you have been drinking heavily for a long time, even though this is a new and exciting situation, it will take a bit of adjustment.

Take the time out to understand *what's in it for you.*

> Remember your love-based goals you set earlier? Take some time to re-acquaint yourself with them now!

We will develop this even more in the next chapter but start to get ready for the success that everyone says is the best thing they ever did.

I have a set of vision cards with my goals and desires illustrated. On them I have the car I want to drive, the holidays I want to go on with my family, and many other things I would love to have show up in my life. Some are 'things' and others are symbols of how I want to be feeling. Some of the things I have on the vision cards have been achieved so I set new goals and some of them are a work in progress. By getting clear on these goals, I raise my energy and prepare to receive their rewards.

It's pretty much inevitable that I will achieve these things because I'm putting so much energy towards them and so much intention behind achieving them, that they almost can't *not* happen to me in my life. You should embrace this too. Getting clear on your goals means you are better prepared for them. You don't get to pick the when or the how, but you can get very clear on the what and the why. You are doing an incredible thing for yourself and you deserve to reap the rewards – whatever they look like for you.

This is a bit like an extension of the love-based goals we discussed earlier in the book. Remember when I mentioned that my sky-high blood pressure normalised within three months of stopping drinking? I realised my heart attack risk factors had dropped by over ninety per cent, meaning I have a good chance of living longer, unforeseen circumstances notwithstanding. I deserve that. My partner deserves that and my children and my, as yet unknown, grandchildren deserve that.

I have never been one for counting days. Some people do this quite obsessively, but generally I am a relentlessly forward-looking person. I know it was a Tuesday in 2016 when I stopped drinking but that is about it. But if that is how you want to measure your success, then go for it, especially in the early days. Over time the power of this fades and you will want to adopt more futuristic goals.

Floor 14 – The Rooftop Garden

You've made it to the fourteenth floor, which is the roof garden on the top of the Tower of Terror. Not so scary was it? It just shows you that with a sound process and a sense of purpose and intention, anything is possible even with things that seemed terrifying.

You can use this model for anything you are feeling fearful about. Fear cannot survive scrutiny. Fear evaporates in the light and thrives in the shadows.

From the roof garden you can look out over your future. By conquering your limiting and disabling fears, you can look forward to feeling better, you can look forward to having more money and to feeling more in control. If you can feel things shifting internally, and want to keep this momentum going with me by your side, you can get the **100-day Momentum programme** via email.

These are daily emails where I will inspire and encourage you on your journey, deal with all the 'practical' stuff, as well as share the successes that I and hundreds of others have experienced. I will talk more on this later – so for now, focus on doing the 'inner work' on your own mindset in order to get strong and confident. These can be helpful as you finish the task of reprogramming your subconscious mind. There will be inevitable bumps in the road and having someone by your side to help you silence the old programmes and associations running in your mind can make the difference between smashing through an obstacle or scraping over it.

Check it out at https://soberinseven.com/momentum

This can be helpful as you finish the task of reprogramming your subconscious mind. So, enjoy the view from the top! Breathe the clean air and feel the wind in your face. At the bottom, this place was shrouded in mystery, and here you are. Well done.

Chapter Review:

Which fears are the most prevalent for you?

What will you do to overcome them?

What support – if any – will you need?

Notes/Reflections

'I have been asked twice at a bottle bank if I owned a restaurant'
Jane, via Facebook

Harriet's Story:

I've been in and out of drinking for so long and I've tried to stop so many times, I've lost count. It has cost me so much physically, emotionally and financially.

It's not just about looks (although drinking affected my skin, eyes, everything) but I've also broken bones (smashed my elbow, broken my wrist). Plus, there is the actual cost, not just of the drink itself but of its consequences... having to pay for new carpets where I'd hit my head and bled everywhere. Drinking demanded I paid a heavy price.

The biggest cost has been relationships. Some I've been able to get back, but others can never be fixed and that's the end of that. There's that awful feeling when you wake up thinking *'What the hell did I put on Facebook last night, who was I criticising, what terrible things was I saying?'*

I didn't drink at all till I hit my thirties, when I met a sociable group of girls. It's hard to know when it went from meeting them for drinks on a Saturday night to something I had to do every day. It was imperceptible, a gradual slide.

In 2010, I went out in the car to buy more drink and passed out at the wheel. How I managed not to kill myself or anyone else is beyond me, but I got arrested and lost my licence. That should have been the wake-up call: I lost my job, it was awful. But because I didn't have to drive, I could carry on drinking. So even that didn't stop me, which is a shameful and shocking thing. I still don't know why it didn't make an impact. I was doing so much damage to myself, but I've come to the conclusion that I just wasn't ready to change.

When I found out about your programme and heard you talking from personal experience, it really rang true with me. I recognised myself in your stories. I too had been through the NHS, to different therapy places where they ask you to list all the drinks you've had and you don't admit to half of it. I'd been to AA meetings and got a bottle of vodka on the drive home. I'd had periods of abstinence then fallen back into the bottle. Nothing had worked for me.

Your videos were great, as I could watch them again and again and see what you had done and how you had changed over time. The 'Future Life' meditation and being able to visualise, looking back at who you were then forward to who you aspire to be, was very powerful for me too. I had a strong sense of whom I wanted to return to. I had lost myself in the mix somewhere. I had become a person I didn't want to be.

When I drank, I also ate rubbish. The programme offered me a different way to live my life. Now my life is all about veg, salads, lean proteins, brown rice, all the good stuff. I now have so many health benefits, way beyond just not drinking. I've also lost loads of weight and I'm seeing it in my blood pressure and cholesterol. It's giving me a powerful sense of wellbeing.

These days, I enjoy getting ready for bed sober and being able to read a book. I feel better, more like the girl from before who was joyful, less complicated.

That joy is returning, reminding me that I want to be part of a community, to use my talents. Singing and dancing have always been a massive part of who I am and I'm re-connecting with them again. Whenever I'm feeling down, I look at the journey I've had, comparing pictures of me when I was really miserable, full of alcohol, bloaty, terrible eyes with how I look now – trim and lithe in a little black dress, banging out a tap dance number with a sparkle and a smile.

Changing my relationship with alcohol has allowed me to find so much more pleasure in life. Now, if you look for me on a Thursday night you will find me dancing on the table, not passed out under it. I'm really living again.

Chapter 5 – Definition

I am about to share with you one of the most powerful techniques I have learned in my life for dealing with ANYTHING that is problematic or troublesome. If you were to put a gun to my head and say, *'Teach me one thing to feel differently about alcohol,'* this would be it.

Now, if you have been browsing through the book and have just read that, you may be tempted to jump right in before doing the preceding chapters.

Don't.

You have made a decision and are investing your time and money – **don't ruin it now!!!**

We are going to do a powerful visualisation technique. The audio is available at https://soberinseven.com/bookresources.

When you experience this meditation as intended, it will BLOW YOU AWAY.

If you are thinking that this kind of thing is for hippies and monks living in caves in Tibet, then I need to engage that open mind that has served you so well this far. Remember the Einstein quote, that problems cannot be solved with the same thinking that created them? You simply cannot reprogramme your subconscious mind without engaging in this stuff.

You actually do this already. When you 'zone out' watching TV, your conscious mind becomes detached, but your subconscious mind is absorbing everything. This is why advertisers pay so much to get their adverts shown during popular programmes when people's guard is down.

You need however to have the insight of the previous modules before getting into this. I have practised this technique a LOT over the last twenty years or so, and it has served me incredibly well.

Remember my story – this is part of the process, and arguably one of the most important pieces. As powerful as it is, it is not and will not be the whole answer.

Don't worry – you will come back to this more than to any other chapter to repeat this and you will not need to even use the audio once you get comfortable with it.

Many of you may be new to meditation/mindfulness, so here are a few simple rules:

1. **Pick a place where you won't be disturbed for a few minutes.** (Quick hint – the loo at work is a great place to do this for a few minutes – and get paid!).
2. **Focus on your breathing.** We generally tend to shallow-breathe ('tidal breathing') and so we use only a small portion of our lungs. The rest of the air can become stale and useless, so simply breathing deeply can boost your energy substantially, as well as creating a sense of calm.
3. **Don't worry about the occasional distraction.** In the busy world, a place of utter solitude and silence is hard to come by. Noises, bangs and voices will inevitably happen, but don't worry, as it doesn't matter.
4. **Practice makes perfect.** Making the busy mind still takes a bit of practice. If you have not done this before you may find yourself flitting all over the place, or at the other end of the scale, losing awareness and nodding off a bit. Don't worry. Any skill or technique needs to be learned and repeated in order to achieve competence. Just watch a toddler taking its first steps.

and most importantly...

5. NEVER, EVER, EVER, listen to this audio when your conscious awareness is needed for tasks such as driving or operating any machinery. Be safe – opportunities to practise this safely are all around you *when you look*.

Let me give you an example of this and how it worked for me.

In 2007 I was up for an industry-wide award. It was the 'Best Picture Oscar' of our industry awards. This was something I was flattered and humbled to have been nominated for, and to be honest, something that I felt TOTALLY unworthy of. My Imposter Syndrome was running rife and I was convinced I was about to be 'found out!'

Nevertheless, it was important to me and also the Good Wolf and the Evil Wolf (see the story I sent you when you entered your details on the website) were tearing lumps out of each other inside me. For several months, I had been visualising the moment. I pictured myself holding the trophy aloft, with a standing ovation from the crowd. I pictured this over and over again and really enjoyed luxuriating in the feelings the images conjured up.

On the night, we arrived at London's Intercontinental Hotel on Park Lane, got our formal evening attire, and went to the function suite. To my horror, I realised there was no stage that I had been visualising so hard and that all the nominees were taken into the middle of the room from where the winners would be announced. I excused myself, went to the bathroom and locked myself in the cubicle, reprogramming the scene with the new reality.

My award was the final one of the night, in true 'Oscars' style. All the preceding winners received a smattering of polite applause from the room, along with a massive cheer from their colleagues on their particular table. The time came for my award. Ten of us were led to the central stage. They announced the third placed individual to polite applause, and then the second. There were eight of us left up there, with the final award remaining. It was all or nothing. My name was announced as the winner.

Unbeknown to me, there were a large number of people I knew in the audience. These were people I had worked with throughout my career who had moved on to other companies and were dotted throughout the room.

When my name was announced, they all leapt to their feet, and their colleagues followed. I received the standing ovation I had visualised so many times and the compere was dumb-struck. When the applause died down, the compere simply said,
'Dare I say, quite a popular winner?'

It was extraordinary – joyous and terrifying at the same time. It made me think, *What have I been playing at all these years?*

The scene played out EXACTLY as I had envisioned.

The following morning, I conducted a similar meditation to the one you are about to do, and the outcome shocked me. I have a boardroom in my mind that I visit regularly. Many influential people sit around that table – sports stars, business leaders and family members. I received congratulations from each and every member of my 'virtual team' and then I came to the final member – my 'higher self'. Instead of getting the plaudits I expected, he simply said, "Happy Now? Move on…"

This insight propelled me forward in my career faster, in the six months following, than I had managed in the previous ten years. Amazing. Enjoy this exercise.

Find a place of privacy, get your headphones on, and enjoy. I guarantee you it won't be the last time you do this. You are about to make acquaintances with the best friends you will ever have...

The Future-self meditation:

For maximum benefit, download the audio and listen to this. If this is not possible for you, then here is the transcription but it is a thousand times more powerful to let me guide you through it personally via the free audio file.

Transcription of the Future-self Meditation:

Perform this meditation sitting in a safe and secure place where you're not likely to be disturbed and never listen to this recording while driving or operating machinery where your conscious awareness is required.

Close your eyes.
Take a deep breath and relax.
Take one more deep breath. Hold it for a count of four.
And relax.
Take one more deep breath. Hold it for a count of four.
And relax.

Feel the way the relaxation is flowing down over your body, starting at the top of your head.

Relax your scalp.
Relax your forehead, flexing your cheeks and your jaw.
So much tension is stored in your jaw.

Relax your neck, your shoulders, your arms, your elbows, relax your fingers, your chest, your stomach, your hips, your knees, ankles, and your feet.
Relax.

Take another deep breath and release.
Breathe normally and deeply.

Imagine yourself on a beach.
You can hear the lapping of the waves. You can feel the sand against your feet and the wind in your hair.
Feel the sun on your face.

This is a place of pleasure and relaxation for you.
Without moving your head, turn your eyes to the right.
You can see a figure approaching.
As the figure gets closer, you start to recognise who this is.

This is yourself, five years from now, your future self who has come to spend some time – to advise and support you on this journey that you have chosen.

As he/she approaches, greet them warmly.

Take a good look at their skin, look at their eyes.

Look at the health that is radiating from them because they have made this journey that you're embarking on.

Ask them for any advice that they may give at this stage.
    They have already travelled this road.
    Listen to what they say.

Take a moment to step into their body. Feel what they feel, feel how your body reacts to the environment that you're in.

Look through their eyes.
    Feel the feelings that they feel.

Take a moment to just look through their eyes and experience that feeling of being in this incredible future self.

Step outside of them once more and thank them warmly for the opportunity to take a good look at what the future looks like.
    Give them an embrace.

Let them know that you will see them again soon. You can come back here whenever you want and as often as you want.

As they walk away, wave to them and know that they are here for you on this journey that you have chosen at any time and you can come back here whenever you wish.

Now again, without moving your head, move your eyes to the left.

Again, a figure approaches.
    This again is your future self from five years hence.

This is your future self that did *not* make the changes that you are planning, and is the logical conclusion of the lifestyle that you are following without any changes.

Take a good look at them.

How do they look to the outside world?
    Greet them warmly.
    Take some time to step inside their body.
    How does that feel?

Perhaps there are some niggling health issues that you already experience now.

How will those feel in five years' time?
    What does their energy feel like?

What does their optimism and outlook feel like, and how does that compare with the future self that you aspire to be?

Step once more outside the body and take a look at them.
    What are the implications that you see for continuing on the path that you are currently on and not making changes?

What does that version of your future self say to you?
    Would they offer you some advice?

Listen to what they say.

Thank them for the time that they've spent here today.

Give them a hug and treat them warmly. This is a place only of love.

Bid your farewells.

You can come back and talk to this potential future self of yours whenever you want and understand the consequences of not changing the path that you're on.

Move your attention back to the beach.

Once more listen to the waves, feel the sand between your toes, feel the wind in your face.

We're now going to come back to conscious awareness again.

As you count slowly to five, on 'one', start to move your body slightly as you start to get some feeling back into your limbs.

On 'two', begin to stretch.

On 'three', begin to prepare for some conscious awareness and to come back to the real world.

On 'four' get ready to open your eyes.

On 'five', open your eyes.

Have a fantastic day. Congratulate yourself for the time that you spent here. Know that this is a place you can come back to at any time and spend quality time talking to and receiving insight from your future selves.

Chapter Review:

What insights did you gain from either of your future selves?

What emotions did you feel as you went through this process? Remember this is an emotional process – we are influencing our feelings in our subconscious. If you felt you skipped through it, then keep repeating this exercise each day – practice makes perfect with this if you are not in the habit of doing this regularly.

Your better future self has been through everything you have been through and has made it to where you want to be. What advice did they give?

Repeat this exercise as often as you can!

Notes/Reflections

Chapter 6 – Opportunity

Now it is time to go back to the Life Balance Disc. You have digested a lot of information, and should be feeling differently with regard to your relationship with alcohol. Have you felt those little shifts? I hope you have been making notes of the things that have resonated with you, and your copy of this book is covered in scribbles.

Remember the combination lock – while some parts of this book may have confirmed what you already know, others should have made you feel challenged and encouraged you to look at things a bit differently. These little shifts in perspective are your subconscious mind taking on new information.

New programmes are now running in that wonderful biocomputer between your ears. That which you have been fighting against is now starting to fight on your side. Some people see alcohol for the lying fraud that it is quite quickly. Others take a little more time. Either way, I hope you are beginning to feel a new sense of optimism and hope. A sense that just maybe this is going to be different.

Most of the people doing the online version of this programme have tried many other things before starting out on this path. If you are feeling completely differently about alcohol maybe your inner sceptic is worried it may be short-lived, or this is some kind of fragile victory. In actual fact, it is neither. This is part of a process. I would love to promote this book as a 'magic pill' that will sort everything out for you, but it really isn't.

You have to digest the contents and do the inner work.

If you are still feeling like you are not 'done' with alcohol, that is OK, but if you haven't yet committed to having your last drink before taking a significant break, then I want you to apply yourself to that now. Use the future-self meditation and the Tower of Terror to diagnose exactly how you feel about that. Are there some fears you have not yet addressed? Is there some intuition you need to receive from your future self?

You can read all the books you want on learning to swim, which is good preparation, but at some point, you have to get wet. Part of this process is to start to experience the alternative to your past behaviours. Going twenty-four hours without alcohol, if you haven't done it for a long time, can feel like a challenge, but remember people do it every day. Millions and millions of people across the globe will not be drinking alcohol today.

If this hasn't been the case for you, don't worry – you may need to experience the alternative reality a couple of times, before the truth becomes apparent.

How has your assessment changed of the scores with/without alcohol?

You will now be seeing a bigger 'gap' between your two potential futures. You now have a far greater understanding of the real truth about alcohol, and will have developed a personal understanding of the unhelpful thinking and associations you have developed over the years. Go back to the Disc and redo the exercise. Give particular thought to the scores you would ascribe to the alcohol-free you. Now that you have had a chance to fully absorb the impact of the non-drinking you, ask yourself – have the scores changed? Were you limiting yourself before perhaps? Take some time to re-acquaint yourself with your new disc.

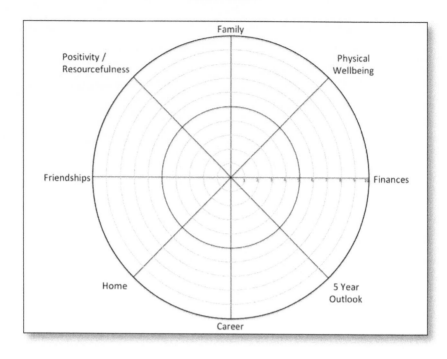

Chapter Review:

You have taken on a lot of new information since you completed your Disc the first time. How has this changed the scores?

Why have some scores changed?

Are you clear on your upsides of seeing this process through?

Do you feel clearer on the downsides of not applying yourself to this change?

If you could write a letter to yourself to advise yourself when you feel you are struggling, what would you advise and why?

Notes/Reflections

Rose's Story:

It's a year on for me now, since doing the course and you know how it is, you just get on with living your life... it takes over. But looking back, it's hard to see past the dark moments.

On the outside, people who met me then and now, might not see that much difference. When I was drinking, I was also a keen runner, up early in the mornings with my friends (nursing a hangover, although they wouldn't have known). I think a lot of my motivations for being really fit then were probably about keeping up appearances (to me and the outside world). These days I'm probably less fit. Instead of relentlessly running, I now walk our two new dogs early each morning (I'd always said no to dogs, but life's too short...) and I'm busy doing other things too. I've just lost the smokescreen: I'm genuinely OK now, not just pretending to be great.

When I was drinking, every day was like Groundhog Day. Each morning I would get up, feeling hungover and awful about myself and worrying about what had happened the night before. Then it would all start over again, the whole groundhog existence with me powerless to change it.

It was so frustrating, as I'm a pretty positive person. I was running, doing well at work, but with the drinking I was just stuck and I couldn't find a way out.

When I found the programme online, I was thinking about it and I remember contacting you, Andy. It was such a surprise when you replied and I think it was that personal response, that care that I got from you when I needed it at the very beginning that triggered me into action.

I thought the programme might help me (which I couldn't actually believe, as I didn't think there was *any* help for me) and I remember you saying *'Just follow the yellow arrows'*. So, I thought *'OK, I'll just do that then.'* I put my faith in it, did exactly what you said at every stage and decided not to question it, not to get too far ahead – just complete one step at a time and that's what worked for me.

The name of the programme is FREEDOM and it works so beautifully because that is exactly what I wanted, I couldn't keep living my life like I was. But it is my way of living that has changed, not me. I'm the same person I always was, but now without the drink and the guilt I can see it more clearly.

The drink and guilt from drinking made me feel that I didn't love my children enough to stop drinking – but now looking back of course I did, I was just stuck. I'm not a different person, but now I have learned different behaviours and ways of thinking. That was really important realisation, that I wasn't bad, it was the drinking that was bad. You think there is something wrong with you when you can't get it under control – and there wasn't. It's an awful lot of years to feel guilty and to feel that you are letting down your family – but I was just the same person underneath, I was just stuck.

Now I've moved on so much, in some ways that drinking life feels like another lifetime. These days, I do some big things I would never have done before, like drive on the motorway, but mostly it's small stuff – we are just getting on with living, getting on.

So, I find it frustrating when I hear things, podcasts and the like, talking about being seven years into recovery and I think to myself how bleak that sounds – how miserable. I'm not in recovery – I'm fine. I'm not being complacent or in denial, I'm really fine. I've dealt with it, I'm true to myself now and I've moved on.

Although I've realised, I'm at heart the same person, many other things have changed. Being sober gave me the clarity and momentum to get rid of a partner who I realised was keeping me down. My relationship with my kids has transformed from doing the programme and I still keep this note from one of them under my bed:

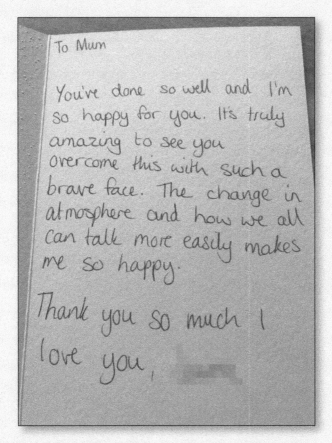

With so much to look forward to, I don't want to keep looking back.

In changing my thinking around my drinking, I've rediscovered not reinvented me – and I've finally been able to say goodbye to that groundhog.

Chapter 7 – MOMENTUM

The Force Field Analysis:

What are the 'blockers' and 'enablers' you will face on this journey? This chapter is all about pre-empting all the obstacles that are going to stand in your way and understanding what you have in your corner. That's going to help you move forward and tackle those things. Forewarned is forearmed!

If we are going to develop a plan to capitalise on our strengths, we also need to work around the things that are going to be a problem for us. So, what I need you to do is to make two lists, as per the diagram below.

Put at least ten things on each list. If this feels like a challenge and you are struggling to get ten, then just keep thinking until you really bring the most that you can out of that creative process. Often it takes a while to get in to the mindset and then the floodgates open!

Let me give you some examples from my own personal experience to give some context:

One of my key strengths is that I am a fairly tenacious individual and I know that there are probably plenty of times in the past that I've displayed tenacity.

I have consistently had that feedback throughout my career and, certainly, while riding the Tour, I leant on this trait on a daily basis.

I needed to think back to those times and to make sure that I could reconnect with those feelings, because there would be times that in order to keep moving forward I needed to rely on that ability to be tenacious.

On the flipside there might be some things that I know are going to be a problem. I tend to suffer from 'imposter syndrome' quite a lot. This is the feeling that I don't deserve to be somewhere, or achieve something.

I often feel uncomfortable and unworthy of praise and have a sense of dread that I would be 'found out' at some point.

This dread was a key trigger for me when drinking and I knew it would come up from time to time, so by identifying it, I was able to recognise it when it reared its head.

Construct your list of ten things on each side of what's going to help and hinder you. The more honest and self-aware you can be at this stage, the more powerful a tool this will become for you. What you will find is that there are some things on the 'help' side that you can then deploy against the things that are going to hold you back. Using the example above, I used my tenacity to doggedly push through my imposter syndrome on many occasions. I sometimes had to adopt an 'I am going to prove this to everyone – especially myself,' approach to avoid me procrastinating and getting stuck.

Using my Tour de France challenge as an example:

While riding the Tour, I had a catastrophic loss of confidence on the sixth of the twenty-one stages and began to really question the wisdom and viability of what I had undertaken.

When we set off in the searing heat of north-western France, for the first three days I was among the slowest of the riders, but there was one group who were significantly slower and less fit than I was and that actually made me feel better.

I am not proud of this, but it actually allowed me to look at what I *had* achieved in my training, rather than fretting over what I felt I *hadn't*.

I assumed they would also finish, and that my training had at least put me in better shape.

However, there was a significant flaw in my thinking.

This group of riders were on one of the shorter loops and were only doing the first THREE days!

Days 4 and 5 saw me right at the back and I started to realise the magnitude of what I had taken on.

I spent two days failing to keep up and my imposter syndrome ramped up to eleven out of ten.

I remember posting a video blog mentioning that I was among the 'racing snakes' of light, lithe, club cyclists and that it was going to be a long three weeks.

Stage 6 was long and hot once more, and finished with two ascents of the infamous Mur de Bretagne. (The 'Wall of Brittany')

I finished the day third last – in front of Curtis who had crashed and was on one of the loan bikes that was too small for him and Stan who two weeks previously had been in intensive care with a punctured lung.

The Stage finished at the summit and the time came to point our wheels back down the hill and get to the hotel.

The descent was straight down and, given that we were a week before the main professional tour, the tarmac was freshly laid and pristine.

Frustrated at my performance over the last few days, I picked up speed and really started to push.

I shot past a few other riders and then had to brake heavily as the route crossed a busy main road at the bottom.

I finished the day shortly afterwards without giving it much thought.

Later, when I looked at my phone to see my statistics for the day on Strava (the fitness logging/GPS app) I was astonished to see that I had made the descent of the steepest part in the thirteenth fastest time *ever*, only four seconds off the fastest of all time!

Isaac Newton wasn't joking when he came up with his laws of motion – large objects carry more energy!

At over 100kg, I was around fifty per cent heavier than the average serious cyclist, and that would serve me well on many a mountain descent in the Alps and Pyrenees.

Upon returning to the hotel (later than virtually everyone else, obviously) I mentioned this to a friend and the news spread like wildfire.

That evening at dinner, this overweight, doubt-ridden and downright slow imposter got a standing ovation from all the 'racing snakes' as I received my award for 'rider of the day'.

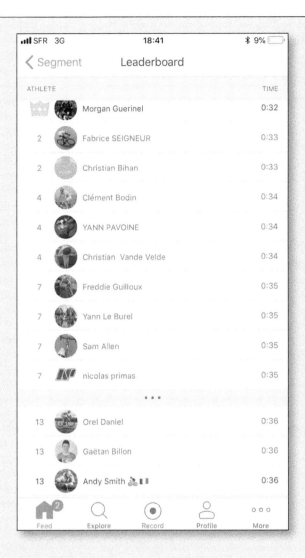

Some of the athletes that I looked up to with such awe came over to ask me what my secret was. They were amazed that I could hit nearly 100km/h in such a short steep stretch of road.

All I could do was shrug, and point at my stomach!

(Before you go thinking I am simply showing off, it is also worth mentioning that for my time going *uphill* on that section, I am currently 2,508th of 2,738 riders...)

By completing this exercise, you are very quickly going to learn how to deploy what you have just learned.

Say for example, you're not great at family gatherings and there are specific people who you know are going to want you to fail in this. It's an unfortunate truth that some people will be less than supportive and you have to navigate through them. Have a think about what your coping mechanism is around that now. You may say you are just not going to attend the gathering, which is perfectly acceptable in the early stages of your progress but a bit of a shame. So, begin to construct your coping mechanisms using this planner below:

Action Plan:

SOBER IN
SEVEN

How I Minimise My 'Blocks':
-
-
-
-
-
-
-
-
-
-
-
-
-
-
-
-
-
-
-

How I Exploit My 'Strengths':
-
-
-
-
-
-
-
-
-
-
-
-
-
-
-
-
-
-

Andy's Top Tip – make sure everything has an action – all threats minimised, all strengths exploited)

Planning ahead leads to fewer shocks. As you go through this you will learn what to expect – the same boring questions, scepticism, etc. But for now some forethought works wonders.

You might want to tell Uncle Jack up front while he is sober that you are on antibiotics so won't be his drinking buddy for the day. He will soon move on to someone else. Having a plan about the upcoming family wedding or the work Christmas party helps keep you on track. With ten things on each side of your plan, you can feel sure that you have given thought to the vast majority of situations you are going to encounter. This is an immensely powerful tool and it helps you really get clear on what the journey ahead is going to look like – at least in the short term while you find your feet.

You'll probably be surprised at how few surprises there *actually* are, now you've had a chance to plan ahead.

Enjoy the process – this is a very empowering thing to do.

Make a note of it in a notebook or on the pages here, so it easy to refer to.

Chapter Review:

What are your key blocks to success? What could you learn from past experiences that haven't worked?

What is going to help you? Think about times in your past when you have achieved things you didn't think were possible – what attributes did you display to make you successful?

Have you got a firm plan you can stick to?

Are there some things that are critical that you need to do in order to be successful this time? What ongoing support will you need?

Notes/Reflections

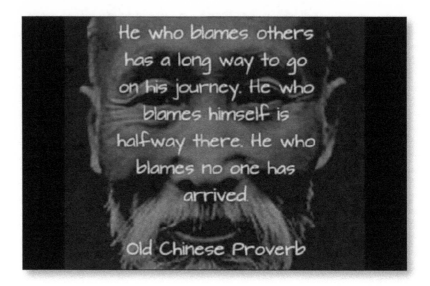

He who blames others has a long way to go on his journey. He who blames himself is halfway there. He who blames no one has arrived.

Old Chinese Proverb

'By the end of the seven-day course I realised I had some control back.

I no longer felt driven to go out, on some addiction-driven autopilot and buy a bottle of wine.

It had seemed as though I had been in a haze, being driven to buy a bottle each day without being fully conscious of my decision.

If I could give up for seven days I could keep going.

I was already feeling the benefits, healthier happier and less anxious. If I kept going this could continue to improve. I had to give sobriety a chance for me and my friends and family.'

Catherine, New Zealand

The Future...

I hope that you have reached this point in the book feeling hopeful, optimistic and focused about what needs to change and how to go about changing it. By now you have the building blocks you need to make a success of this. Your combination lock is unlocked and you are ready to open the door to your future.

You are returning to a place of peace and tranquillity with regard to the role alcohol plays in your life.

Stepping off the conveyor belt of addiction allows you to marvel at just how intertwined an addiction to a poisonous substance can become in your life.

Society has gradually programmed your subconscious to a place of helplessness and it has destroyed your self-esteem. Now the fight back begins!

As you walk among the people who have not yet had your awakening, you may begin to feel frustrated that the conspiracy has become so widespread. You may want to help others, now you have seen the truth. That is a wonderful thing to do and I would argue that it is the vital next step in your healing process. People will watch you. When you don't fail or crumble, they will seek you out. You don't have to force it on them or even judge them.

Before your own awakening, you would not have responded to that, but you would have taken note of someone who had been a role model about their drinking and that would have been intriguing to you. So, when someone asks you about it, they may well be struggling and not feel able to admit it, even to themselves. Remember this is a journey from guilt and shame to love, kindness and joy. Addicts wallow in the former, so be a beacon of hope in the latter.

I often get messages from people who are frustrated with ridiculous social media posts or alcohol promotions. These are the reasons people get sucked into this trap – it is subtle, insidious and gradual. And it is not going to go away anytime soon, unfortunately. But now you know different. You see it for what it is.

This is not a problem you can fix single handed, but when people seek you out for help and inspiration, be kind and give them some of your time. You are the leader; you are the inspiration and you are the strong one. You may have heard this story:

One day a man was walking along the beach when he noticed a boy picking something up and gently throwing it into the ocean.

Approaching the boy, he asked, 'What are you doing?'

The youth replied, 'Throwing starfish back into the ocean. The surf is up and the tide is going out. If I don't throw them back, they'll die.'

'Son,' the man said, 'don't you realise there are miles and miles of beach and hundreds of starfish? You can't make a difference!'

After listening politely, the boy bent down, picked up another starfish, and threw it back into the surf.

Then, smiling at the man, he said... 'I made a difference for that one.'

I hope this book has set you on the path to a most wonderful destination. You are not there yet, but you are on your way. You may now be thinking, 'What next?' and wondering how you capitalise on this new feeling of momentum.

I hope you want to continue to build your alcohol-free future and I hope my story has inspired you to get some further support as you explore your new reality over the next three months. You can access a 100-day email programme which I have specially prepared for people who are keen to move forward with their lives.

In this programme I will send you:

- practical, proven strategies on how to deal with the realities of your new future, such as what to tell people or dealing with social events
- powerful personal developmental tools to turn your new-found energy and time into things that massively increase your happiness and joy
- further reading to build on some of the themes in this book
- exercises and structure to make your new-found sobriety a permanent part of the joyful you
- an opportunity to interact with me personally via email.

I get so much positive feedback about this email programme; it is a pleasure to offer it to you at a discounted price as the reader of this book.

Simply visit https://soberinseven.com/momentum and enter code SISBOOK to receive your discount.

I look forward to seeing you on there, and would be thrilled to join you on this important next step of your journey. You don't have to do this on your own, and you don't have to work it all out for yourself. It is probably the part of this process I get the most feedback on, and indeed many of my clients tell me that having a steady guiding hand through the first few months was what 'did it' for them. By receiving these emails, you are tapping into my experience, and the experiences of thousands of others just like you who are creating a better life for themselves and for those around them.

I look forward to chatting with you.

Big Hug,

Andy

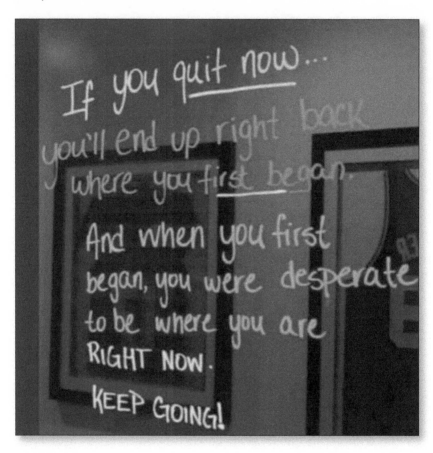

Notes/Reflections

Lightning Source UK Ltd.
Milton Keynes UK
UKHW040618230120
357484UK00001B/260